DILEMMAS AND CONTRADICTIONS IN SOCIAL THEORY

G. Llewellyn Watson
University of Prince Edward Island

UNIVERSITY
PRESS OF
AMERICA

LANHAM • NEW YORK • LONDON

Copyright © 1987 by
University Press of America,® Inc.

4720 Boston Way
Lanham, MD 20706

3 Henrietta Street
London WC2E 8LU England

All rights reserved

Printed in the United States of America

British Cataloging in Publication Information Available

Library of Congress Cataloging-in-Publication Data

Watson, G. Llewellyn.
Dilemmas and contradictions in social theory.

Includes index.
1. Sociology—Methodology. 2. Frankfurt school of
sociology. I. Title.
HM24.W284   1987   301'.01   87-21570
ISBN 0-8191-6638-3 (alk. paper)
ISBN 0-8191-6639-1 (pbk. : alk. paper)

All University Press of America books are produced on acid-free
paper which exceeds the minimum standards set by the National
Historical Publication and Records Commission.

ACKNOWLEDGEMENTS

I am deeply indebted to the Senate Research Committee, University of Prince Edward Island, for financial support which made possible the research on which Chapter 2 of this book is based. The Committee's support at the stage of final manuscript preparation is also hereby acknowledged.

I thank Judi MacKinnon, secretary to the Department of Sociology and Anthropology, whose competence and skill with the word processor made the task of writing this book relatively easy. Many thanks to Wilma Robinson for her assistance with the index.

May 1987   G.L.W.

Contents

Acknowledgements — iii

Preface — vii

INTRODUCTION — ix

CHAPTER ONE
Key Issues in Modern Social Theory — 1

CHAPTER TWO
Understanding Patriarchy: The New Challenge to Marxian Theory — 19

CHAPTER THREE
Positivism and the Roots of Critical Theory — 45

CHAPTER FOUR
The Critical Project — 67

CHAPTER FIVE
Ideology As Social Discourse — 109

CHAPTER SIX
Critical Perspectives on World Capitalism — 131

CHAPTER SEVEN
Dilemmas and Contradictions in Social Theory — 149

CHAPTER EIGHT
Understanding Black Society: Dilemmas and Contradictions — 169

Index — 187

PREFACE

Sociology might quite reasonably be defined as the attempt to understand social issues. Students who read sociology at university often confess that after three or four years of being exposed to sociology the fragmentary and incoherent knowledge of social issues which they brought with them to the university is not added to in any substantial way. Many of the key social issues of our time, such as struggles between rich nations and poor ones, the awesome power of economic organizations, the pillage of the Third World, poverty and world hunger, sexual and racial oppression, remain dimly understood, inspite of our claim to possessing abundant scientific knowledge. Many of these issues remain oddly shrouded in a haze of vague theories. As well, capitalism seems to have stabilized itself in the wealthier countries. Yet it is precisely in these countries that we find high and seemingly permanent levels of unemployment and inflation, economic crises, and grinding poverty in the midst of affluence. Most of the sociology books read by the students fail to deepen their understanding of these issues, as well as the contradictions within capitalist society.

These original essays utilize the theoretical framework provided by critical theory to analyze several of these substantive social issues. As in the earlier volume, **Social Theory and Critical Understanding** (1982), the major aim is to demonstrate how a social theory can serve as a crucial medium for illuminating and elucidating many kinds of social experience which we confront in everyday life. The primary aim of these essays, as of all sociology, is to provide a clear view, historical interpretation, and an accurate understanding of ourselves and our times. Social theories only become useful when they can be applied to practical social issues.

The essays in this book explore the social, philosophical and ethical implications of sociology, and indeed of any attempt to understand the relationship between social theory and human activity. In many ways, they are locked in a programmatic fashion in an engaged debate with what has been termed the 'orthodox consensus' of contemporary sociology. It will be argued throughout that social theory's usual uncritical perspective on modern society is fundamentally one of the major reasons for the lifelessness and pedantry of which sociology as a whole has long been accused. These essays are aimed at encouraging fresh thought and reflection on the critical study of society, and at using theory to put some life back into sociological analysis, to probe for a better understanding of the social world we live in. Moreover, they seek to do so by recognizing the need for critical evalution and re-alignment of social theory itself. The reader will find throughout this book pointed reference to, and critical discussion of, dilemmas and contradictions in social theory, as well as within the structure of modern society which theory seeks to explain.

INTRODUCTION

Theoretical works abound in sociology. But theoretical understanding is not commensurate with this abundance. Most of these works are of American origin, and a good number stem from Europe. Theory books which make reference to the Canadian experience are much more rare. Social theory concerns human societies, wherever they are, and a conceptual framework, if it is at all useful, ought to have relevance for different societies that show similar structural features. Yet, more and more it seems, students lodge the complaint that much of what they read as social theory fails to reveal how society works and reproduces itself. They declare, sometimes with good reasons, that their comprehension of the historical and contemporary forms of industrial society is sabotaged by mystification and abstraction. Much of the theory which is presented fails to provide conceptual tools that convey a sense of the structural unity of important sociological issues.

Writing from within the U.K. in 1984 sociologist Ian Craib remarked in the opening pages of his book **Modern Social Theory** that:

> The very word 'theory' sometimes seems to scare people, and not without good reason. Much modern social theory is either unintelligible, or banal, or pointless. The reader does not feel she is learning anything new or anything at all; there is certainly no excitement. Even for the specialist sociology student or teacher, it requires a lot of hard work with the minimal result of simply being informed ...[1]

Craib goes on to point out that on top of all the difficult problems and pitfalls in producing theoretical work, the teaching and learning of social theory itself operates within, and helps to create, a peculiar mystique which in turn creates a disturbing environment in which to study. The problems of obscure language, grudging respect from some colleagues, and barely veiled hostility from colleagues and students, are there **before** we even start the journey. It makes the journey a perilous one indeed!

'My guess' Craib concludes, 'is that most people start (this journey) because they have no choice. It comprises a compulsory course at some stage in their student career, and they grit their teeth and get on with it.'[2]

Social theory therefore finds itself in a paradoxical position. There is no way we can dispense with it or avoid it if we are interested in enlightening men and women about the institutional sources of their social existence. Yet theory is seldom enjoyed, is often despised, and more often than not 'appears to be scholastic dialogues, sermons or alienating polemics ... On sociology degree courses theory is often the most apparently irrelevant and tedious area for students. This is because theory has become divorced from practice in the discussion of theory itself.'[3] Thus sociology fails students not because of the way it is taught, but because what is taught is all too often drained of practical implication, so that the potential of sociology as an approach which could help people achieve an analytical grasp of their problems is lost.[4] In this way, too, theory tends to lose its grip on practice and misses its mark as a potential medium of social criticism.

The essays brought together in this volume address some of these concerns. But they are also written with the knowledge that by far the most common criticisms brought against social theory is that much of what is being done **as theory** is simply a rehash of old ideas and widely known research. This is an easy criticism to make. But the key question of whether we can **transcend** some of the 'old' ideas, given that we have **not** gone beyond the circumstances that gave birth to them in the first place, is often overlooked. One is likely to be castigated for not 'saying anything new.' In Canada, one is likely to be told that so-and-so said it before, or made the point with greater sophistication x number of years ago; or worse, that this or that idea is not relevant to a 'decent society' such as Canada. Perhaps because of this ethos, Canadian publishers no doubt with the conservative Canadian academic community in mind, continue to shy away from the publication of critical and theoretically oriented studies.

One hears and encounters criticisms often enough that this or that idea would have been relevant two decades ago, but not today. For serious consideration, theoretical ideas have to be 'new.' The key point is often missed, namely, that we might offer understanding rather than mystification if we isolate some of the 'old' ideas about human society and **interpret** them in the context of our time. In short, maybe there is more to be gained from asking **new** questions about old issues for which satisfactory answers were never provided, than with forever chasing new trends without having gained one answer in earlier attempts.

Social theory is important because it is inevitable. 'If there is one thing which is as certain about our lives today as the intellectual impossibility of taking modern social theory wholly seriously, it is the absurdity of hoping simply to dispense with it.'[5] The fundamental question, then, is how we might demand of a conception of social theory that it be a potentially emancipatory critique of society, and that it concerns itself not just with scientific methodology but with asking new questions. For 'it is the asking of new questions that leads to new knowledge, and this is the hermeneutical element of all knowledge, including science.'[6]

There is no great abundance of evidence to suggest that we have offered yet the sort of theoretical critique of modern capitalist society that could inform social and political practice, and provide the basis for a more rational normative order. It is the aim of these essays to provide a sketch of some of the social factors which define, contain and stabilize the social existence in modern society. For this task, there is no abiding interest in devising abstract theoretical principles, or in searching for invariant laws of social behavior. Rather, the interest is in interpreting the social knowledge we do have in the context of the changing world that we have had a hand in creating. We apply knowledge when we have systematically interpreted the meaning of ideas against the backcloth of history; when, in short, we have given the concepts of social analysis a structural unity that is homologous with the world as we actually experience it.

It is the goal of social theory and the single key characteristic of any serious social theory, to render the world as we do experience it comprehensible. The problem which, it seems, has long haunted sociologists is whether we can in fact do that in the absence of some set of 'laws' of human behavior. The essays in this book demonstrate how we might attempt that: how we might make sense of the experience of social life and shed light upon some basic human concerns.

Social theory can be understood as a way of asking questions about society in ways that must allow us to reach beyond our present selves. Social theory understood in this manner implies that a theoretical grasp has within it a mirror of utopia, of better worlds to what is; or has the potential to heighten critical consciousness, thereby increasing our understanding of the possibilities for change.

The sociological project is at bottom a theoretical project. To investigate reality, we need a clear theoretical perspective or framework to serve as an interpretive scheme and as an organizing schema within which to discipline brute facts. Our theories must explain the facts. Then, to the extent that a theory or a perspective helps us to explain ourselves, to bring order and coherence to the wide range of social facts, and to understand why things are as they are, it will, sooner or later, have practical and profound utility.[7]

Any social theory worthy of the name has to be intensely concerned with two fundamental sets of relationships; or what I rather like to think of as two dialectics: one, the relationship between human beings and nature; and two, the relationship between human beings and society. Grasping these, and understanding the possibilities for change and for history-making inherent in them, is what we **most need to know** as a result of our analysis of human society. Grasping these is the key to the understanding of the genesis and structure of **any** social order. Ours is a capitalist social order, and this carries a significant implication. This type of social and political organization does not, as a general rule, make readily available to those who would study it, the social and cultural foundations on which it thrives. This makes it all the more necessary for a social theory for our time to be a particular kind of critique. Such a critique must be based on analysis.

Because sociological theorizing is a certain way of thinking **about something,** and a certain way of looking **at something,** we have identified certain features within the structure of capitalist society that demand our attention. If there is any merit to the idea that sociology can help to bring enlightenment to human beings, and so help them change their world, logic requires that we should first understand that world. And understanding it further requires that we do not become so cautious as to hide behind difficult realities. Or worse, use the belief in the impossibility of agreement about painful issues as a way to avoid discussing them.[8]

Ideology in sociology is one of those issues that tend to be given short shrift in social theory, even though it is a **process** which, if understood, can open up new horizons of theoretical understanding. This concept, then, runs through all these essays and provide the necessary connecting link between what might otherwise appear as unrelated processes. Ideologies are an integral part of social and political struggles, and are rooted in an overall system of class and power relations probably in all heterogeneous societies, and most definitely in capitalist ones. Alvin Gouldner depicted the problem for sociology when he claimed that sociology is more ideological and less purely scientific than it claims, and ideology is more rational than its opponents give it credit for, both being modes of discourse or responses to the newly problematic nature of reality in post-traditional society.[9]

The essays in this volume speak to this unhappy conclusion. But they also entertain the optimism that if we are to probe into the nature of modern society, as it actually is, we must examine rather more deeply the character and consequences of ideology as discourse, as a particular form of human thinking. Our aim, in brief, is to essay empirical understandings of the world and the human situation by, as much as possible, lifting the mystical veil that cloaks society and inhibit our comprehension of it.

NOTES

1. Ian Craib, **Modern Social Theory: From Parsons to Habermas**, Brighton, England: Wheatswaf Books, Ltd., 1984, p. 3.

2. **Ibid.**, p. 5.

3. Joe Bailey, **Ideas and Intervention: Social Theory for Practice**, London: Routledge and Kegan Paul, 1980, pp. 16-17.

4. **Ibid.**, pp. 20-21.

5. John Dunn, "Social theory, social understanding, and political action," in Christopher Lloyd (ed.), **Social Theory and Political Practice**, Oxford: Clarendon Press, 1983, p. 115.

6. Christopher Lloyd, "Introduction," **ibid.**

7. Janet Chafetz, **A Primer on the Construction and Testing of Theories in Sociology**, Itasca, Ill.: F.E. Peacock Pub. Inc., 1978, pp. 9-13.

8. See Barrington Moore, **Reflections on the Causes of Human Misery and Upon Certain Proposals to Eliminate Them**, Boston: Beacon Press, 1972, p. xi.

9. Alvin Gouldner, **The Dialectic of Ideology: The Origins, Grammar, and Future of Ideology**, New York: Seabury Press, 1976, pp. 19, 35.

CHAPTER ONE

KEY ISSUES IN MODERN SOCIAL THEORY

I

Following upon the initial observations and comments made in the Introduction, this chapter outlines a broader theoretical project in the sense of identifying some of the crisis points in modern social theory. These points account for some of the key issues in modern social theory. Subsequent chapters take up some of these issues and theoretically flesh them out in the context of the nature of capitalist society in the 1980s.

Sociologists wish to be scientists. This goes back, of course, to Comte, who conceived sociology principally as a positivist social science capable of providing high level empirical propositions as the basis for accurate prediction and control of social phenomena. Perhaps this is the first curse of sociology. Everywhere one looks in sociology books, one finds the claim that sociology is a science. But often this claim is made whether or not it is understood that this science might possibly attend to practical social questions. In fact, one often gets the distinct impression that the claim is an excuse for **not** attending to practical social questions.

Herein lies an important difference between Comte and the theoretical heritage deriving from him. With Comte, sociology was to be a positivist science, but also considerably more than that. It was to be a new critical discourse on politics and society, a probe into the new and troubling times and the concomitant system of values of post-Revolutionary Europe. From its very beginning, sociology was tied to social and political problems; not just scientific ones.

The question of why unemployment is sorrowfully high in the world's richest and most prosperous nations is a **social** question which can be understood without invoking formal science. It is also a **social** question when politicians in the rich liberal democracies openly

Dilemmas and Contradictions in Social Theory

declare that we can no longer afford to pay for social programs, yet they devote more and more resources to prepare for wars, or to start them. And must we appeal to science to tell us why the homeless live alongside and forage in the refuse heap of the sophisticated? Or why multinational corporations enter Third World countries and somehow convince the local politicians and the peasants that instead of growing beans or corn or lentils, they will be better off to turn to 'cash crops' needed in the overdeveloped world: rubber plants, cut flowers, coffee, tea and carnations? The claim to science in sociology, alas, is often a claim to be neutral, objective and unbiased, to be unconcerned about how knowledge about society is used, an excuse, as we said, for not attending to practical social questions.

For all its scientific pretensions, liberal sociology, that is to say mainstream, orthodox sociology, has not developed the kinds of conceptual tools capable of understanding, in a structural sense, many of the major human concerns of this period of the twentieth century. It can be argued of course that there is nothing which the sociologist can do about such matters, for the issues call for political action. The sociologist does have the responsibility to provide analyses which show the human roots of such experiences. As sociologists, our critical understanding can help to provide more adequate perceptions of the nature of the social world. Our contribution can be given in the form of deep incontrovertible analyses of the nature of modern society, displayed in the form of our uncovering of social facts that had not hitherto been known. If we have no adequate analysis, it is not because we are incapable of providing one, but because we have consistently refused to take into account certain concepts and categories, indeed certain **experiences,** which could potentially produce deep, relevant insights and understanding. Sociological theory has always suffered from the tendency to accentuate certain partial truths and myths, while at the same time denying the possibility of alternative interpretations. Maybe this is peculiar to all theoretical systems. Even if that were so, the time is ripe to examine our social myths rather more closely. Myths may be very comforting indeed, but they do not as a rule come to grips with reality.

We must seek to comprehend what it is about

Key Issues in Modern Social Theory

sociology that predisposes it to assume that some social questions should not even be considered in analysis. Is it due to the fact that perhaps much of modern sociology is probably cast in ideological terms? There is evidence to suggest that it is on ideological terms, rather than on substantive or logical ones, that, for instance, Marxian analysis has been effectively kept out of academic sociology for such a long time, especially in North America.[1]

For those who have drawn upon and utilized Marxian concepts in social analysis, there can be no doubt about the authenticity of the Marxian paradigm as a comprehensive framework for understanding capitalist societies. The contributions of Marxian theory to the development of Western scholarship have only now been (somewhat begrudgingly) acknowledged. As Aronowitz puts it, Marxist scholarship is now taking centre stage in many areas of the humanities and social sciences. It is no longer possible to ignore it or pretend that it is not a powerful theory for comprehending the social world.[2]

In the absence of Marxist contributions, sociologists have matter-of-factly wallowed in the ignorance of liberal theory as it has ambled along, explaining things superficially, enlightening too few. As capitalism advances from one agonizing structural crisis to another and as the multiple ideologies of racism, sexism, scientism, consumerism and others beg for explanation, liberal theory anxiously wishes that ideology would end. In effect, the very conceptual area of ideology, and ideological debates, in the tradition of North American sociology, have become something of sociological lepers, studiously avoided by sociologists, as though they were harboring contaminants guaranteed to disfigure sociology.[3]

Clearly, to the extent that there are ordinary people who would like to grasp some of society's pressing realities, but who receive no deep insight from orthodox liberal theory, there can be said to be a crisis in the understanding of modern society. Between the treacle of liberal economics, the impressionism of standard sociology and the emptiness of political rhetoric, there is little which truly makes sense or coincides with the lived experiences and reality of ordinary citizens, and very little indeed about the political and economic forces that shape their lives.

Dilemmas and Contradictions in Social Theory

It is fully recognized, of course, that the idea of 'crisis' in sociology is not new. Since the 1960s, sociologists both in the West and in some socialist countries have lamented the crisis or the 'coming crisis' in sociology.[4] But beyond the crisis which these earlier accounts noted, the essays in this volume focus sharply on the theoretical analysis of aspects of modern society that touch all our lives. The question is whether these can be understood or rendered understandable by others besides academic sociologists. The crisis in sociology is a crisis in understanding; it is a crisis rooted in sociologists' entrenched timidity in spelling out what a theory of society in our times should be, or can be.

Sociologists are, unfortunately, not known for always turning the searchlight onto their own activities and assumptions. To that extent, it is entirely possible that the dilemmas and contradictions, not to say crisis within sociology, are only dimly recognized by sociologists themselves. In fact, as we show in subsequent chapters, this is largely the case. Sociologists who write theory books continue to languish in the barren domains of positivism, blissfully salivating for a science of society that will not be critical, or which will not generate critical reflection, but which would somehow be 'precise.' The crisis deepens each day we fail to give a unified account of the course of history which renders that history comprehensible to ordinary citizens. Those of us in the teaching business are aware that the frustration is felt every day by students, who have, in turn, wondered how it is possible for seemingly inadequate 'theories' to persist.

What lies at the heart of the crisis in liberal theory? Its deep-seated conservatism and lack of a sharp historical sensibility are by now well known. It is too often the case that liberal theory takes the status quo as given, and does not seek to transcend either conceptually or empirically the ideas and actions relating to its acceptance at any given time. One can quite easily read into liberal theory the idea that things are as they are because of human's basic nature. Hence one of the strongest ideological supports for capitalism is the way the theory which 'explains' it generates a belief in the necessity and eternality of this arrangement, and of the theory's own persistence. The Sociology which grew out of the

Enlightenment was not unanimously critical of some of the more negative consequences of the new era, and of the human implications of the transformation from feudalism to capitalism.

The liberalism in Weber's sociology pushed him, as we know, to the point where he was forced to equate capitalist rationality with rationality per se, and to conceive of industrial society as an inevitable bureaucratized and unstoppable juggernaut, created by human beings, but incapable of revision or intervention by them. Weber's position is not very different from what some modern popularizers of sociology have to say. Alvin Toffler, in his **The Third Wave** is very much suggesting (in a neo-Weberian style) that more and more bureaucracy, more and more robotization, inflation, unemployment and other unpleasant things are coming at us (in the name of rationality?) and there is nothing we can do about it. This is the worse sort of determinism. To subscribe to such a scenario is to acknowledge that our understanding of society as social arrangements, indeed, our grasp of history, is in crisis.

Two possible responses to this liberal vision come to mind. First, it is entirely possible that late capitalist societies are continuously producing human problems, many of which simply will not be solved by the standard bureaucratic means, if in fact their solution is seen as necessary. Second, the gloomy image of the Third Wave clearly reflects the impressionism of liberal theory. For if we in fact conceptualize humans as subjects who make history, and not just as passive objects of inevitable laws, the future would look quite different from that portrayed in 'Pop' sociology. The future would be taken as something not just to be predicted, but to be decided upon by men and women who have made themselves aware of the status quo and the options available for changing it.[5] In Sarte's terms, the future would take the outline of a project to be accomplished. Or perhaps Kant put it best when he said that we can prophesy the future only to the extent that we bring it about. To be able to do that, we must comprehend the present with all its built-in contradictions, something which liberal theory does not seem to have accomplished, to judge from their recent record (see Chapter 3 below).

Where we seek an understanding of any situation that is in principle explainable, but are faced instead

Dilemmas and Contradictions in Social Theory

with mere puzzles, we can say that there is a crisis in understanding. For instance, the tyranny of liberal economic theory makes it difficult for most of us to transcend the visceral recitation of the virtues of modern society, or to imagine that we can shape the social future to what we ideally want, and are capable of achieving. Such an economics, with its 'rational' model of human behavior in the marketplace, bears little relation to the reality of capitalist speculation, where people speculate in everything from comic books to international currency, displaying behavior which seems the opposite of what most of us do normally as rational people. The practice of international speculation such as that which is carried on at Stock Exchanges often seems to defy basic logic. In fact, it becomes highly questionable whether such behavior constitutes rational human conduct, or collective madness. If it is madness, it is one in search of profit, riches and self-aggrandizement.

II

The Marxian theoretical system has as one of its major concerns human historical possibilities. In Marxian social analysis, the categories isolated for analysis are historically grounded, and the logic of analysis used to account for human experiences always seeks to anchor itself in history as human praxis; that is, in the concrete historical situation of human existence, especially in the ways in which human beings actively produce their social and material world. Even so, there is little doubt that Marxism, especially Western Marxism, is itself today in the midst of an historical crisis, not simply within the movement, but of Marxism itself. We shall return to these later.

For the moment, it should be remarked that what gives Marxism its cutting edge is the way it seeks to reveal real relationships hidden or mystified in phenomenal forms, and the way in which it reasons that no social arrangement is inevitable, fixed for eternity, or beyond question. This is the essence of his analysis of the fetishism of commodities, of class struggle, and of ideology as that which tends to universalize the partial. When Marx picked a quarrel with the classical political economists of the nineteenth century, it was on the charge that those scholars engaged in false abstractions, considering

Key Issues in Modern Social Theory

some aspect of economic life such as production, as completely separate from the total set of social relationships within which it is placed. This way, the classical political economists immortalized the relationships they described, presenting contingent historical facts, for example the form which labor takes under capitalism, or the relations which lie behind commodity exchange, as eternal laws of nature.

This is the crux of that important concept of **reification**. In a reified consciousness, there is no historical remembrance. Thus, not only do people tend to feel powerless and awed by humanly-created structures and relationships which they do not understand; but they see these relations and structures as somehow fixed, given, and eternal. In brief, they mistake the historic and social with the natural, and the specifically social appears as a physical thing. Thus, in the case of the classical political economists, despite their great knowledge of historical change, the classical political economists nevertheless gave ahistorical accounts of transient and condition-specific social relationships.

Marx's broadest theoretical project was centred around the problem of how to dissolve the error whereby people forget that the social and cultural worlds are humanly constructed, and therefore changeable. For him it became a major philosophical and social question of what happens when a physicalist ontology resulted in a systematically generated distortion of social reality. On these counts alone, Marxian theory cannot be taken as just another point of view, but as a comprehensive conceptual framework inspired by a critical analysis of class societies.

The crisis in Marxian theory has come about inspite of Marx's attempt to offer an extensive and thoroughgoing analysis of capitalist societies and to reveal their structural tendencies. The crisis dramatizes a central feature of social theory, namely, that as a critical reflection upon society it can never be a completed project. It reminds us to expand and refurbish an already substantive framework, to use it to think creatively about contemporary social and political issues and situations. Many elements of Marxian social theory have become historically obsolete; many others are as valid and as profound as when they were first formulated. We do not abandon or discard a theory of society because it fails to account

Dilemmas and Contradictions in Social Theory

for all the twitches and movements in an historically unfolding **human** situation. Rather, we try to understand what conditions within this **situation** would endear human beings to make the kind of history they do, and why.

One of the most important issues contributing to a crisis in Marxism concerns an ongoing reflection as to why the expected revolutionary subjects -- the working class in industrial societies -- have not emerged as key players in drama of social change. This query is particularly sensitive to orthodox Marxism which has to grapple with the fact that it was mostly the middle-class youth, along with Third World minorities, and not the working class in any shape, new or old, that called for an end to capitalism in the turbulent 1960s. Given this fact, it is not surprising that some critics, such as those of the Frankfurt School, have virtually abandoned, or at any rate severely diminished the role of, the proletariat as the likely agents of social transformation. (There is further discussion of these points in Chapter 4.)

Following upon the humiliating defeat of the German working-class by Nazism, and, in other capitalist societies, the seeming integration of the working class into capitalism, a sort of pessimism has crept into Marxian theory. This has caused some scholars, such as Habermas, to argue against Marx, in order to point up that the altered structure and dynamics of late capitalism calls for a radical rethinking of Marxian categories to account more fully for such realities as the new strategic role of the modern interventionist State, the new meaning of political domination, and the multi-layered crisis in industrial society; and, of course, the failure of radical proletarian consciousness.

There can be no question but that the modern State is partly responsible for disguising class interests and class conflicts, thus preventing the fundamental contradictions within capitalism from igniting radical praxis. Similarly, the dovetailing of science and technology in advanced capitalism effectively conceals the relations of domination in a society constructed of class inequality. These themes are explored further in later chapters of this book.

A second type of crisis within Marxist sociology concerns the important problem of racial and ethnic and

Key Issues in Modern Social Theory

sexual oppression within capitalist social structures. Considering the historical importance of racial and ethnic groups to the birth and subsequent development and expansion of industrial capitalism, Marxist theory is not as clear-cut as one might expect on the subject. Marx's writings, and those of subsequent Marxists, have shed some light on this matter. The widespread use of 'imported' labor in many of the affluent societies in Western Europe, and of almost exclusively immigrant labor in some industries in North America, such as in the garment industry, in the factories and in the home, are classic examples of modern-day class-exploitation.[6]

The major difference between the present situation which exploits immigrant labor and Marx's original formulation of class oppression, is that the former has a distinctly ethnic/racial dimension. A plurality of ethnic groups comprises this labor pool; Marx's classes were basically homogeneous entities. The immigrant-ethnic exploitation parallels the history of western colonialism and ethnic oppression which the advanced capitalist societies are known for. The oppression cuts two ways when the capitalist class from the advanced capitalist societies exploit the labor and resources of the Third World. On this point, it has also come to be something of a sore point in Marxist theory that unfortunately even existing socialist societies are not altogether free from ethnic conflict and/or oppression.

In sum, in whatever version it might be applied, Marxist thought lacks a treatment of racial/ethnic discrimination as a source of exploitation independent of class domination. The two are quite different issues in modern societies, and Marxists have yet to produce analyses of ethnic discrimination on the same scale as the traditional preoccupation with class. The formal study of ethnic stratification and ethnic exploitation in modern cosmopolitan societies must be conceptually linked to the broader analysis of social inequality. The trouble with traditional studies of stratification in society is that more often than not, the assumption of ethnic homogeneity was freely made. That assumption is no longer valid in the plural systems of North America and Western Europe.

A third issue amounting to a crisis within Marxism is that of sexual oppression. It is well known that Engels, in his **The Origin of the Family, Private Property and the State**, addressed himself to the

9

question of the oppression of women in relation to the rise of capitalism. But Marxist theory, especially of the orthodox variety, has not accounted adequately for the origins and nature of sexual oppression in the modern world. In the absence of a concern for the oppression of women (until fairly recently), liberal theory has so successfully rationalized the domination of women in ideological terms that few now consider that that domination is anything more than invariant 'human nature.' The lack of understanding of the oppression of women in capitalist societies has clearly presented Marxist feminists with a challenge, and the signs are that a crisis of this type will bring forth an eventual enrichment of Marxist theory through analysis, critique and theoretical extension.[7] It is perhaps true to say that even the critical theory of the Frankfurt School had not, in its early phases, anticipated the dynamic feminism of the current period. The theme of patriarchy or male oppression constitutes the discussion in the next chapter.

A fourth point concerns Marx's critique of culture. Marx did not develop a full-fledged critique of culture, and because of this lacuna many Marxist scholars, beginning of course with Lukacs and Korsch, and including many within the Frankfurt School, have argued that modern Marxism must include in its swath a sustained critique of science and culture. Their point is that Marx, for all his brilliance, and perhaps because of his preoccupation with a critique of economics, paid too little attention to the possibility that advanced capitalism would develop cultural accoutrements and techniques aimed specifically at absorbing or de-stinging the potential protest and criticism of modern publics. Hence, the cultural apparatuses of modern capitalist societies such as manipulative advertising, deformation of language and the occlusion of consciousness through cultural distractions, are not to be thought of as unimportant, but instead as constituting some of the key structural features of contemporary capitalism, to be analyzed, understood, and transcended.

To the extent that Marx offered a discussion on ideology, he never completely overlooked the cultural problems of capitalist societies. His analysis of ideology is inadequate and misleading only because it is ambiguous. More than he ever imagined, capitalist societies conceal their own constitutive social relations and built-in contradictions. It is not so much that all the structural features which Marx explored have vanished, they are simply concealed. Marxist theory must continue to reveal the truly human dimension of contemporary capitalism.

This idea connects up to a final crisis, even a frequent lament, that the Marxist theory of the State is grossly inadequate for coming to grips with the modern interventionary State of the twentieth century. The harshest version of this lament from the Left is that we don't have a theory of the State such that would expose with theoretical clarity the conditions of advanced capitalism, conditions which require the State to assume a range of new functions, including internal repression, not discussed or anticipated by Marx. In works by Nicos Poulantzas, Louis Althusser, Ralph Miliband, James O'Connor, among others, we see enormous theoretical efforts and preoccupation with filling this gap and with formulating the theory and reality of the State in advanced capitalist societies. Something that would have interested Marx is revealed in these expositions, namely that the modern State is obviously caught in a contradictory situation, from which it finds it difficult to escape, given the underlying imperatives of such a State: wanting to manage economic growth; yet heavily dependent upon wealth generated privately, and hence wealth which it does not directly administer. Modern Statism seems, if not well equipped, at least prepared to manage, any and all the crises and contradictions inherent in capitalism. Given the nature of some of these crises, it is very possible that modern capitalism cannot continue to manage them and maintain its present formation.

Two fundamental implications derive from this reality. First, the modern State presents itself as its own political legitimizing force and the unity of the nation. But in doing so it accomplishes another end. Even while dealing with social relations in capitalist society which are by definition class relations, the modern State's definition of persons as individuals obscures their distribution into classes. Thus another paradox of the capitalist State, as Poulantzas suggests, is that it is structured with the absence of class, while capitalist society is in fact class society.

The second implication is that the intervention of the State in liberal capitalism is explained in terms of liberal theory. Such a theory opaques the social

Dilemmas and Contradictions in Social Theory

whole. Individualizing social experience is a task well accomplished by liberal theory and its accompanying ideology. This helps to explain why people continue to accept what they suspect to be false, and continue to live in social conditions and under social arrangements they recognize as exploitative and oppressive. Indeed, it is one of the triumphs of liberal ideology that it manages very well to convince the majority of people in society that the existing system is eminently fair, just and equitable, working to the mutual benefit of everyone. Accordingly, if there is 'failure,' it cannot possibly be explained in systemic terms, but in individual terms. The failure, in short, is due to personal and individual shortcomings. The liberal ideology of 'equality,' 'individualism,' 'free choice,' 'universalism' form the bedrock of the capitalist State. Such an ideology first of all legitimizes the status quo; secondly simplifies a complex social reality; and thirdly distorts the very nature of class/capitalist society.

There will be further discussion on the State in a subsequent chapter. For now, it must be carefully noted that this crisis in Marxist theory is not to be perceived as the end of Marxism, or as a condition that demands its abandonment, any more than the crises within capitalism have not engendered its end or its abandonment. The dialectical interplay of description and critique, and the possibility of achieving alternative realities by informed social practice, form the essence of the Marxian theoretical framework. The fact that Marxism has had to re-examine some of its major premises in the light of historical changes and shifts in the twentieth century, is not a 'refutation' of the theory. As in the case of capitalism being able to face and overcome one agonizing crisis after another, and even being fortified by them, so, too, Marxian theory can benefit from a critique of its shortcomings and oversights. Indeed, it is to Marx's credit that the theoretical framework which he developed to analyze the structure of capitalist society still today facilitates a comprehensive critical analysis of the very historical developments that make the updating and expansion of his theory necessary.

III

The foregoing brief notes point up that, in a number of spheres and on a series of issues modern social theory, including Marxism, faces a crisis in understanding. One must conclude that throughout its history, crisis has been endemic in sociology in that there has never existed within it a consensus as to what it is, what it can be, or what it ought to be. That in itself amounts to a key issue and concern in social theory. But perhaps the most fundamental social question of all surrounding this dilemma has never been disputed hotly enough, namely, the question of the critical macro-understanding of modern capitalist society. If what we say we have understood about society is all there is to understand, then we have in social theory several missing links, for human struggle is still not rendered understandable by the most popular theory in sociology - liberal theory. We need to seek comprehension through both self-reflection as well as reflection on reality in its broadest possible shape. And even more than that, we need to take the observables of daily life and weave them into a sensible framework which not only shows how they belong together, but what they mean for humanity and history. Social theory cannot be exhausted until history ends. The point then is not just to cast the social world in a scientific mould, but to understand it.

The problematic for modern social theory, as it clearly was for Marx's critique of political economy, is how to enable ordinary men and women who are not politicians, jurists, priests or professors to thoroughly understand their situation and possibly transcend it. Given the particularity of their standpoint in the first place, and given that they do not directly control the generation and/or dissemination of ideas and modes of thought, ordinary people are subject to distorted communication, to use Habermas's phrase. The challenge to cultivate what Habermas terms an ideal-speech situation is worthy of all our intellectual endeavours and energies. This idea is further elaborated in Chapter 3.

The kind of appeal made by Arthur K. Davis some seventeen years ago to academic sociology in Canada to develop macrosociological and holistic approaches[8] toward a Canadian sociology, is still relevant today. This was a call to develop a structural sociology that would lay bare the major structural features of the society we live in. It was a call premised on the observation that the prevailing paradigms in academic sociology came nowhere close to addressing the vital questions of class conflict, the nature of capitalism, or the history and consequences of imperialism. Unfortunately, half a generation later, many of the puzzles which Davis identified still remain as puzzles, hidden in the fog of liberal theory. It is doubtful whether, as a result of doing theory, we are any closer in the late 1980's to understanding capitalism than we were in 1970, although advances made in such areas as feminist scholarship have been impressive.

Understanding the capitalist pulverization of human social relations on a global scale is a necessary task of social theory. The task cannot be accomplished unless and until we operate with a theoretical concept of capitalism as two things at once: as a stage of economic development; and as a structure of social relations. To comprehend the second of these two aspects, with all the modern human and institutional implications, requires no less than a radical break with much of the thinking hitherto accepted as 'sociological theory.' By far the most outstanding feature of the social relations of capitalism is the reification of all human relations. On this, the cultural Marxists such as Lukacs and Marcuse have given us points of departure. The contemporary social theory of capitalism must continually seek to renew itself on the challenge of these pointers.

As for Marxism, renewal there requires some radical rethinking and reconceptualizing of the relationships between politics, philosophy and culture in such a way that cultural politics becomes an integral part of all that theory aspires to, and cultural criticism becomes political criticism. Perhaps, paraphrasing Pascal, we might conclude that the minute we doubt sociology is the minute we begin doing it.

The essence of Marx's (partial) critique of sociology was essentially the problem of how to cultivate the creative consciousness which ordinary people need as an antidote to the permanent entrenchment of dominant ideologies. Marx did not present such a program in any extensive way, but he nevertheless insisted that one must do everything possible to expose the fact that classical political economy had a predilection to sever the differently conceived modes of knowledge so that a total grasp was inhibited, and an objective account precluded. This problem is still with us.

Bourgeois economics, like liberal sociology, is not straightforwardly either wrong or untrue, scientific or ideological, so much as it represents systematically distorted structuring of reality in which the vital historical dimension of that reality is left out of account. The systematic exclusion of any concept of historical totality and the occlusion of historical possibilities encourages the fetishtic reification of human social relations into timeless 'laws.' It is thus that economic theory assumes that the so-called law of supply and demand determines price in the marketplace. It is as though conscious price manipulation, planned scarcity, and the **ideology** of multinational agribusinesses or pharmaceutical conglomerates are not worth considering. Small wonder that economists, for all their flashy models and paper-sophistication, have not explained one of humanity's most threatening experiences - world hunger - never mind finding a solution to it. What these models usually retain as their vital parts is notably less significant than what is left out. Classical economics, like liberal sociology, thrives on the myth of neutral science, and produces, accordingly, not explanations of the real world of inequality and human injustice, but a rationalization of it. To the extent that such rationalizations are accepted as some sort of unavoidable destiny, society as a whole is prevented from understanding the irrationality of the dominant system of legitimation.

The remarks in this chapter constitute the registering of radical doubt about modern social theory. Doing social theory must come to mean fine-tuning a substantive critique of liberal theory as ideology, as a justification of capitalist practice falsely given in the name of community and 'human nature.' The depth of this illusion is still undisclosed in the theoretical explanations of the modern world with all its pathos, incongruities and lop-sided sense of priority. A critique of liberal theory involves theorizing the human agent, as mirrored from real existence. And the distinctive contribution of the social scientist should be his or her consistent, unswerving application of critical intelligence to the status quo, to grapple with the larger, more serious issues of our time even when these resist precise formulation, measurement and clean-cut

Dilemmas and Contradictions in Social Theory

profiles, and even when we risk the ire and scorn of our scientific colleagues.[10]

In the next chapter, one of the issues traditionally ignored in Marxian and traditional sociology alike - the question of patriarchy - is given some theoretical exploration. As with the other essays in this volume, attention is directed to the need to tighten critique, and to address the problem of ideology as it has helped to shape our view of the world in the modern period, including our theoretical explanations of contemporary society.

Key Issues in Modern Social Theory

NOTES

1. See, for example, Richard Flacks and Gerald Turkel, "Radical sociology: the emergence of neo-Marxian perspectives in U.S. sociology," **Annual Review of Sociology**, vol. 4, 1978, pp. 193-238; Parick J. Garvey, "Historical origins of ideological denial: the case of Marx in American sociology," **The American Sociologists**, vol. 16, 1981, pp. 196-201; David Sallach, "What is sociological theory?" **The American Sociologist**, vol. 8, (3), 1973, pp. 134-139; and Julia and Herman Schwendinger, **The Sociologists of the Chair: A Radical Analysis of the Formative Years of North American Sociology**, New York: Basic Books, 1974.

2. Stanley Aronowitz, **The Crisis in Historical Materialism: Class, Politics and Culture in Marxist Theory**, New York: Praeger, 1981.

3. G. Llewellyn Watson, "Review of M. Patricia Marchak's **Ideological Perspectives in Canada**," in **Canadian Review of Sociology and Anthropology**, vol. 20 (3), 1983, pp. 375-78.

4. See, for instance, Alvin Gouldner, **The Coming Crisis of Western Sociology**, London: Heinemann, 1970; and Tom Bottomore (ed.), **Crisis and Contention in Sociology**, London: Sage Publications, Ltd., 1975.

5. Kenneth Westhues, **First Sociology**, New York: McGraw-Hill, Inc., 1982, p. 13.

6. See, for instance, Laura C. Johnson, with Robert E. Johnson, **The Seam Allowance: Industrial Home Sewing in Canada**, Toronto: The Women's Press, 1982. These authors have, in this unique book, exposed the raw capitalism and exploitation which takes place in the garment industry in this country. According to the authors, the $3 billion garment industry in Canada employs about 100,000 homeworkers, 75 percent of whom are women, and most immigrant women, who, in the words of June Callwood (back cover of book) 'toil for the garment industry and make dresses on a piece-work basis — for about $1 apiece. This is the underbelly of capitalism which most of us associate with the 19th century, not the Canada of

1987. This hidden labor force, like the Black domestic workers in Canada, together reveal more than any other form of labor (except perhaps farm laborers) the heartless exploitation of human labor for profit maximization. And the fact that in both industrial home sewing and in domestic work there is so much secrecy, raises questions about the conditions of work, and the structure of relations between the workers and the employers.

The factory side of this industry is no better, as revealed in a series of investigative reports in the **Montreal Gazette,** April 25, 1987. After having put herself in what she termed Dante's Inferno world of the immigrant factory workers', applying for 41 jobs and landing three, and having worked in their sweatshops for the minimum wage, she reported that many immigrants are working in conditions that others would not accept, conditions that make their noses bleed and their ears ring with the deafening roar of production. Always, they must please the boss, including the boss's sexual harassment. To refuse meant being fired or having to quit. And quitting looks bad to the immigration officials (p. A-4) (cf. Makeda Silvera, **Silenced:** Talks with Working Class West Indian Women About Their Lives and Struggles as Domestic Workers in Canada, Toronto: Williams-Wallace Publishers, Inc., 1983).

7. Richard Kilminster, **Theory and Practice in Marx and Marxism,** in G.H.R. Parkinson (ed.), **Marx and Marxism,** Cambridge: Cambridge University Press, 1982.

8. A.K. Davis, "Some failings of anglophone academic sociology in Canada: the need for a dialectical and historical perspective," in Jan J. Loubser (ed.), **The Future of Sociology in Canada,** Montreal: Canadian Sociology and Anthropology Association, 1970, p. 31.

9. For more on the question of reification as it manifests itself in modern society, see G. Llewellyn Watson, **Social Theory and Critical Understanding,** Washington, D.C.: University Press of America, Inc., 1982.

10. Westhues, **op.cit.,** pp. 16-17.

CHAPTER TWO

UNDERSTANDING PATRIARCHY: THE NEW CHALLENGE
TO MARXIST THEORY

I

For all his interest in structures of domination in capitalist society, Marx never confronted squarely the question of the domination of women by men, nor seriously questioned the hierarchical **sexual** division of labor in capitalist society. Rather, he accepted it to some extent as dictated by nature, and criticized capitalism for failing to recognize such differences.

Marx's apparent disinterest in patriarchy seems to be connected to the assumptions on which he operated. He assumed (1) that the material basis of patriarchy lies in precapitalist modes of production; (2) that subordination and oppression in capitalist society was essentially the same for men and women, deriving from the same source and understandable in the same structural terms of proletarian oppression; (3) that the inner logic of capitalism is antipatriarchal in that the capitalist mode of production undermines the family, and thus the traditional site of patriarchal authority; and (4) that the subordination of women and the possibilities for their liberation could only be adequately comprehended if we proceed from the assumption of the primacy of production. In a word, in Marxism, 'women are seen to inhabit only capitalist relations, rather than both capitalist and patriarchal relations.'[1]

As a result of these multiple assumptions, Marx could shed little light on the problem of patriarchy. Neither he nor Engels fully grasped the hierarchical sexual division of labor and its implications for the reproduction of capitalism, even though the thoroughgoing analysis of capitalism was their primary concern. Engels, in fact, provided some early insights into the emerging position of women in capitalist society, and saw that the oppression of women by men was distinct from class exploitation.[2] Indeed, he noted that the primary division of labor was that

Dilemmas and Contradictions in Social Theory

between the sexes, and referred to the privatization of female labor as the domestic enslavement of women. But he stopped short of a thorough analysis. Like Marx, Engels failed to explain the labor process **within the family** or to draw out the implications of the vested interests men had in women's confinement to housework as unpaid labor. In the words of Heidi Hartmann, then, the categories of Marxism are 'sex-blind.'[3] The socialist tradition has never adequately addressed the question of women. Given Marx's overall interest in, and concern for, oppressed groups in society, it is curious that his neglect of patriarchy is so pronounced.

Patriarchy is a fundamental system of domination, described as that condition in which men define women as inferior, and in which women are obliged to conform to that definition. It is a sexual **system of power** in which males possess superior power and economic privilege; it is a social and economic arrangement, the material basis[4] of which is men's control over women's labor-power, and, we would emphatically add, over their **fertility** and sexuality as well. Hence the control is, at the very least, double-barrelled. The institutionalization of housework under capitalism, as labor which is not paid for, but which nevertheless fulfills key functions for capitalism, suggests exploitation in the classical Marxist sense of extracted labor-power not being paid for by those who benefit from it. Exploitation is found in any structure of the relations of production which generates alienated labor.

In connection with this question of labor, three important observations are worth commenting on. **First,** capitalist job segregation by sex - the division between private and public spheres - relegates women to housework, and by **cultural practice,** to the characteristically lower paid gender-defined paid jobs. This arrangement assures women's economic dependence on men, and reinforces notions of appropriate spheres for men and women.[5] **Second,** women are (actually or potentially) **reproducers** of children who become workers for the economy and members of the society. This way they perform labor for men as well as for the productive system. **Third,** women also socialize these children for their roles in the work world and the society as a whole. They labor to feed, clothe, and care for their husbands and these children. In short, women in housework serve as domestic laborers within the economy, and as nurturers of the social world, not to mention serving as 'expert' consumers.[6]

By all these multiple praxis, domestic work helps to perpetuate the existing society, to stabilize patriarchal structures, and to reinforce notions of appropriate spheres for men and women. As Secombe puts it, at the economic level the housewife's labor reproduces on a daily and generational basis the labor-power of the worker, and at the ideological level it reproduces the relations of dominance and subordination required by capitalist production.[7] But there is an argument, which Janet Sayers calls 'misguided feminism,' which holds that women can achieve equal status with men by being confined to domestic labor (if they are paid for that labor). This is to be rejected as shallow, or as Sayers says, as an argument which fails to serve the interests of women.[8] The question of **why it is women** who are exclusively assigned to the private sphere to perform such labor would still have to be addressed.

The most fundamental point in all of this is frequently overlooked. It is that the system of privileges, the benefits **to men,** and the profits accruing to the economy 'could not be organized as such if the **ideology** and structures of male hierarchy were not basic to the society,'[9] organized and delivered at the level of popular consent and imbibed uncritically. Ideology is basically the protective cocoon beneath which exists the relevant structures and factors of domination and exploitation. Ideology functions to manipulate reality in ways which serve particularized interests - mainly those of men - rather than universalistic interests. Domination therefore implies specific historical distortions of labor and interaction which arise in the course of history, but which are explained away in ideological terms. To the degree that women are excluded in a wholesale fashion from the public sphere and from full participation in the labor force, they are not part of the working class struggle, and their liberation is thereby unduly stymied. Perhaps there is merit in Adrienne Rich's and Shulsmith Firestone's thesis that women are a **sex class,** or Morgan's idea that women do in fact constitute a separate social class.[10] In any event, traditional Marxian analysis only considers the paid working class; the mass of unpaid labor which **women** exclusively perform is not fully accounted for.

Dilemmas and Contradictions in Social Theory

Although ideology is the topic of a later chapter in this book, it is important, and necessary, to briefly discuss ideology here, since one of the major claims of this chapter is that the understanding of patriarchy is best approached via a firm grasp of ideology and ideational constructions. Marchak describes ideology as a screen of assumptions, beliefs, explanations, values, and unexamined knowledge about realities, held by its very nature by faith.[11] As such, an ideology is a mode of thought and of discourse. But it is also, in class society, the expression of a world-view of a given class or group, used to justify or rationalize the political or social interests of its advocates. It is not an unconscious system of thought, but rather a highly integrated, if shorthand, conception of the world. In practice, ideologies tend to be convincingly simple, seductively straightforward, rather than sophisticated; and this is part of their appeal and attraction. They reduce the complex world of social relationships to a few simplistic concepts. Designers of dominant ideology always work toward making ideological signs uni-accented; in other words, to have accepted the myth that things cannot be any different from what they are, since it all has to do with 'human nature.' Thus, for Mannheim, as for Marx, (as we shall see later), ideologies were inherently **conservative**.

Marx felt that ideologies were more often false, because they were partial, representing only the points of view and interests of those who create them. One of his major concerns was to criticize the way such partial knowledge nevertheless claimed exclusive authority and validity at large. In fact, Marx was at pains to point out how as mobilizing and integrated belief systems, ideologies served to consolidate the existing social condition with justifications derived from the status quo. Thus they effectively shield existing society against its own historical alternatives and necessarily obscure social processes and cultural practices. In bourgeois economics, for example, the ideological character of the wage form is never questioned, and hence Marx points us to the illusion, that the laborer's wage is claimed to be 'fair' and 'just.' That makes sense ideologically. Non-ideologically, it is equally easy to claim that there is no just price for labor. In fact, it could be said that capitalism is a ruthless and cruelly inhumane method of production which thrives on the exploitation of the worker, paid or unpaid. Such an interpretation is never seriously entertained by those who would view capitalism as an eternal verity, or as the ultimate perfection of which human beings are capable.

As a putative body of 'knowledge' which is interest-bound, **patriarchal ideology** operates in such a fashion as to conceal some key social relationships. To the degree that it functions to obscure the nature of the relations between women and men, it helps to prevent the realization of historical knowledge and hence the possibility of social transformation. The ideology generates a belief in its own necessity and its own eternality, elevating the partial and the historically specific into 'natural,' immortal laws of nature. The social blinders which such a belief creates, and the determinism which it promotes, in turn serve to stabilize a given social arrangement. In such circumstances, the major sociological questions are, simply, how to comprehend the taken-for-granted assumptions that underpin daily practice; and how to dissolve domination if it is not even recognized? It is difficult to change intellectually or socially what is not socially given. All ideologies, from religion to sexism, racism and free enterprise, have an element of myth, and this Marx recognized. The essential task of social theory is to dissolve the myths through critical analysis, and expose the structures of beliefs and practices which often work in the interests of those who contributed the mythical component in the first place.

Given these problems, there are good theoretical grounds for insisting that the understanding of patriarchy is best approached from the vantage point of ideology and ideology-critique.[12] One of Marx's lasting discoveries was that all ideologies originate within social practices and arise out of the necessity of social problems. Ideologies do not, and cannot, arise independently of social structure. As Harris puts it, the study of ideology can most usefully be undertaken in the context of a consideration of culture as a whole rather than in an isolated fashion. Ideologies are not disguised descriptions of the world, but rather real descriptions of the world from a specific viewpoint.[13]

Dilemmas and Contradictions in Social Theory

II

That Marx could have explained the dynamics of capitalist society as well as he did without adequately disclosing capitalist patriarchy, is a curious anomaly, puzzling, given the close intertwine between patriarchy and capitalism, and given Marx's penchant for laying bare the 'laws of motion' in capitalist society. Patriarchy and capitalism are cleverly intertwined, but they are not identical. Feminists have pointed out that to the extent that patriarchy is a structure that performs functions on behalf of the capitalist mode of production, the fate of patriarchy is ultimately bound up with the fate of capitalism. As Eisenstein and Beechey, among others, note, capitalism uses patriarchy and patriarchy is defined by the needs of capital.[14] Let us note here two important things.

First, at the level of cultural practice, patriarchal relations bolster capitalism, just as capitalism sustains patriarchy by projecting the myth that the private sphere of labor is unproductive and insignificant. The myth is not easily revealed. Capitalism's reified form of objectivity is well known. Indeed, one of its signal successes as a structure of social relations is its ability to utilize ideology to justify its imperatives, at the same time as it systematically obscures its own inner workings. Its economic data are given, and taken, as 'natural' facts, quintessentially cases of the relations between things.

Second, patriarhcal structures have succeeded in consolidating the widespread **belief in** both patriarchy and capitalism, and in the ideology of the naturalness of the sexual division of labor. To the degree that the sexual division of labor and the concomitant male economic and social privileges are not questioned theoretically or in practice, the aspects of domination inherent in such arrangements are maintained. Aronowitz sums up this situation well when he says that women are dominated ideologically as well as physically to the extent that they become convinced that male power is rooted in nature and is therefore just.[15] The **appearance** of naturalness gives patriarchal domination the image of a 'law of nature,' a factor which helps the domination to sustain itself.

Even some feminists are themselves victims of this ideological fog. Thus, one finds, among so-called radical feminists, the argument that patriarchy is rooted in biology - in women's unique, if oppressive biology, and specifically in their reproducctive selves[16] - in other words, in the fact that women mother and nurture. Biology, it is said, has favored women with a special instinct to nurture and care for children,and, by implication, suited to the domestic sphere.[17] This position, widely accepted by men and women, feminists and non-feminists, extends to the point where the demarcation between men and women is suggested in a simple formula: men = culture; women = nature.[18] Culture devalues nature; therefore men devalue women. This suggestive, if vulnerable idea from Sherri Ortner could easily be taken as a firming of biological determinism. Ortner adds, however, that it is not biology as such which explains the apparent fixity of women's social subordination, but the **social attitudes towards** female biology, a complex which Elizabeth Janeway labels social mythology.[19]

In short, women's subordination is due to the **ideas** society entertains about their biology. Such ideas are cultural products, even in a patriarchal society, and they are therefore changeable. They are never to be understood as immutable, fixed, biological givens. It is the **social construction** of sex differences which is crucial.[20] This is a problem in the sociology of knowledge. Ortner's idea is vulnerable because she seems ambivalent about the distinction between biology and culture and in the end she leans toward accepting the immutability of culture itself. According to Janeway, we may not even be dealing with a fact of biology so much as with a male-constructed social mythology, a distinct set of normative ideas intended to consolidate a particular world-view and to sediment specific values.

To say that male domination is rooted in the biological difference between men and women, whereby men, (because of aggression which is determined by male hormones), have captured power by force in order to ensure privileges,[21] is to reduce the complex question of culture to trivia, and to court a fallacy. This view is soundly criticized by Janet Sayers,[22] but we would further add that if men have done any dominating, it is not so much because of biology. Rather, the domination is ideational. The biological argument seems curiously similar to the 'human nature' fallacy which Marx discovered in Feuerbach and against which he delivered his famous polemic in Theses on Feuerbach. It is an argument that denies the fundamental

25

Dilemmas and Contradictions in Social Theory

historicity of all social characteristics and projects them instead as immutable, ahistorical social formations. It creates the sort of mysticism and determinism that is fodder for the sociobiologists.

From a sociological point of view, what is important is not the sexual/biological difference in society, **but the ideological and political interpretations given to that difference.** As Eisenstein remarked, women are not oppressed because of the biological fact of reproduction, but by men who define this reproductive 'capacity' as a function.[23] Women **do** have the unique biological capability to bear children, but over and above that, men have traditionally not seriously considered that **they** could rear children, even after the breast-feeding stage is past. Only now is this attitude slowly changing. Women's oppression, clearly, depends on a number of elements created by their situation of straddling two worlds: home and work; and of being caught in the contradictions produced by both. And, contrary to Engels and traditional Marxism, women's entry into the paid labor force has not saved them from male oppression. The continuation of this oppression is revealed by such experiences as the sexual harassment of working women, the double-day work pattern, rape and domestic battery.[24]

A second feminist fallacy revolves around the origins of patriarchy. Here the contention is that capitalism is the cause of women's oppression, and of their being forced to stay at home as nurturers and child-care specialists. This is a favorite thesis of liberal feminists,[25] but it is not at all tenable, because it has not been supported by the available evidence. Capitalism is not the cause of this situation; patriarchy is. The strongest case in support of the objection comes from the empirical observation, documented in the anthropological and sociological literature, that all societies which have been reliably studied are partriarchal.[26] This system of domination not only predates capitalism, but it is analytically independent of the capitalist mode of production and distribution.[27]

The subordination of women continues in societies where there has been social transformation of the relations of production. If that is so, the subordination **is one of women by men** and not simply by a given mode of production. What is interesting here

Understanding Patriarchy

is the observation, outlined for instance by Szymanski, that the Yale Human Area Relations Area files, as culture-bound as they are, conclusively demonstrate that the social and political position of women in preclass societies was qualitatively more equalitarian in relation to men than it has been in class societies.[28] The structures of male power and privilege (which are also the structures of female oppression) may appear timeless and unchangeable, but they are, we submit, socially constructed, and hence susceptible to human analysis, intervention and transformation.

There is obviously a transhistorical character to male domination, but the degree and nature of this dominance have varied, perhaps considerably, in time and place. Additionally, there is now ample evidence that patriarchy cuts across different political systems and modes of production. Women's oppression occurs under socialism as much as under capitalism, and women under contemporary socialism are confronted with the reality of the double-day of work. They experience patriarchy in a form not unlike the women under capitalism.[29] Any simple equation of patriarchy with capitalism, or of capitalism with women's oppression is therefore inadequate.

The persistence of a male-dominated sexual division of labor in contemporary socialist societies immediately undermines the theory that capitalism is the exclusive source of patriarchy in the contemporary world.[30] But the feminist point is well taken. Only by struggling against capitalism will we be able to shake up the dominant assumptions of men as a whole, so that these assumptions can be flushed out into the open and problematized in theory and new practice. Only in the process of struggling against oppression can people formulate new visions of alternative realities and structures. The fact that patriarchy and capitalism, as two analytically separate structures, have coexisted in such harmony over time and place is clearly a major sociological issue with which we must come to terms. But the analysis must also seek to account for the sources of patriarchy in non-capitalist countries. Any easy equation of patriarchy with capitalism or with women's oppression, is to be resisted as inadequate.

In summary, these points bear repeating: Capitalism and patriarchy are two sides of the same dialectic of domination. In capitalist societies, the domination is such that what is almost totally obscured and forgotten is the fact that the specific form that patriarchy assumes under capitalism performs decisively important functions for the reproduction of this mode of production[31]. This is not a simple 'functionalist' theme. The domination of women is a logical **extension** of the domination of nature, the **raison d'être** of capitalism since the Enlightenment. Capitalism provides a material basis for patriarchy, not **the** material basis, as some feminists have argued. Capitalism is not the exclusive source of women's oppression; patriarchy is. This is why it cuts across cultures and different modes of production. Neither Marx nor Engels showed us how these two systems of domination conceived of and responded to women as factors of production. Yet, to the degree that male domination is institutionalized and made an aspect of the 'natural order,' feminism's future is assured, for feminism is nothing if it is not a struggle against patriarchy.

III

Marxism is a comprehensive theory of the genesis and structural dynamics of capitalist society, including the underlying class contradictions in such a society. But if Marxism is to continue to make sense of the modern world, its orbit must be extended to deal with patriarchy as a sexual division of labor within and outside capitalism - as a structure of oppression with cultural rather than biological or purely economic roots. But we should not expect that Marxism will necessarily provide all the answers we seek; merely that in this context it can become more useful. Three key points must be noted here.

First, if Marxist theory will insist that the capitalist mode of production is the material basis of patriarchy, it will fail to explain this reality. A purely economic explanation does not explain the paradox that, given the relative cheapness of female labor, their participation in the labor force is dramatically lower than that of males. Furthermore, it might even be argued that traditional Marxist theory does not explain, and has no theoretical framework for understanding, the sex-specific forms of oppression **within** capitalism: sexual harassment, prostitution, rape and battery. All of this suggests that we must look not to the interest in maximum surplus value extraction, but rather to an extra-economic interest for an adequate explanation. If patriarchy persists across a number of different modes of production, then it cannot be understood to be a function of a particular mode of production.[32]

Second, if we cannot empirically and logically conclude that patriarchal domination is the result of the existing mode of production, then it follows that the transformation of this same mode will not (necessarily) guarantee the elimination of the domination which patriarchy is. Now, if patriarchy rather than capitalism is in fact the source of women's oppression, even the most radical analysis of capitalism, such as that offered by Marxist theory, might not be sufficient to explain the culturally defined sexual division of labor, or to increase our understanding of this fundamental form of domination. In fact, we would argue that patriarchy is not understandable via the 'mode of production' approach, but via the spheres of sexuality and procreation - more via the mode of **reproduction**. This is why patriarchy cuts across different economic systems or modes of production. Its universality is rooted, we suggest, in the sexual objectification of women in most, if not all societies, and the power men have had over **reproduction and sexuality**.

Third, Marxian theory has proved inadequate in explaining the origin and persistence of patriarchy because Marxism has no critique of everyday life, 'the core of which is the patriarchal character of sexual relations' in which women as nature remain subject to men.[33] Here, the feminist project is significant. The feminism of the 1960s and 1970s, unlike earlier versions, can be seen to have been an effort to bring Marxism to judgment, in that, as never before, the attack on male domination within the sphere of everyday life - the personal - was of paramount importance. By describing and openly challenging the way in which male domination manifested itself and was reproduced within our most intimate activities, feminists demonstrated convincingly that the 'personal is political,' and that the liberation of women would require a transformation of the innermost structure of male-female relationships that had hitherto been understood to be 'beyond politics.'[34]

The feminist position is certainly a key one from

which to call, once more, for the interrogation of what Lukacs calls the 'antinomies of bourgeois thought,' those abstract dichotomies between fact and value, subject and object, freedom and necessity, theory and practice, knowledge and interest, culture and nature, the public and the private, science and ideology, the personal and the political - essentially patriarchal dualities which theoretically fragment and distort a view of the whole so as to make it unintelligible. The apotheosis of these false splits must never go unchallenged.[35]

The power of feminism grows out of contact with the cultural practice of everyday life, and out of struggles to comprehend, and possibly transform everyday life: sexuality, interpersonal relations, ideology.[36] By insisting that the personal is political, the feminists registered that what goes on within the domestic realm is not purely 'private trouble' but 'public issue' (to use C. Wright Mills' elegant phrases), legitimate subjects for open public analysis and discussion. The politicization of personal life remains one of the notable achievements of feminist theory.

Neo-Marxist theory, such as that associated with the Frankfurt School, and the works of Habermas in particular, seem to be taking a turn away from the mode of production assumption, to other spheres which Marx neglected, for example, the critique of the culture industry, and to a theory of distorted communication. (See the discussion in Chapter 3)[37] Clearly, the Frankfurt School's attempt to get beyond Marxian theory by opening up discussions on such topics as domination, the influence of mass culture on consciousness, and the sustained critique of ideology, is to be welcomed. Building essentially on Lukacs's concept of **reification,** some members of the School, such as Marcuse and Horkheimer, have forged a social theory which moves towards a critique of the institutions of everyday life, for example, schools, family, mass culture, and advertising, precisely the arenas where the ideology of patriarchy is psycho-socially introjected.

On a more basic, but important level, the challenge to Marxian theory is to return to a serious rethinking of that complex, protracted primary process - the cultural process of **socialization,** and specifically what capitalist institutions require of this process.

Understanding Patriarchy

That challenge wants us to investigate the set of social relations which structures the production and reproduction of everyday life, including the production of sexuality and the gendered definition of women's work, which give rise to sex-specific forms of women's oppression. Because these relations are both capitalist and patriarchal, the challenge is that of simultaneously exploring capitalist ideology and patriarchal ideology as twin forces of women's oppression. The power of social theory, as a critical reflection upon society, lies in its ability to creatively and reflectively forge a dialectical unification of the antinomies of thought previously mentioned. That way, we can then move from fragmented, reified thought to the understanding of totalities.

Feminists have exhaustively described and condemned the way in which the family, the mass media, and other institutions of socialization. Specifically, they wish to understand how such institutions contribute to the reproduction of the structure of domination within which, in one way or another, women are obliged to 'put up and shut up,'[38] and accept as destiny the female-dominated childcare, their alienation from culture, and alienation from their bodies.[39] By their reasoned condemnation of male privileges, the feminists have given needed fillip to theoretical analysis, and they have reshuffled our critical intelligence. The way in which they have announced their judgments on patriarchy signals a return to a theory that is critical of social arrangements, and to a conception which recognizes that because patriarchy is cross-national does not also mean that it is inevitable.

No social arrangement is inevitable; ideological constructions often represent given social arrangements as natural and inevitable. Modern feminism has sensitized us to the dangers of such a claim. In doing so, they have shown how socialization may be, in reality, the most subtle, if effective means of mediating domination in human societies. Accordingly, they strike a chord, which Marx would not have minded: 'all science would be superfluous if the outward appearance and the essence of things directly coincided.'[40] The (necessary) feminist critique of male domination is also, one might add, a challenge to Marxist scholarship to closely seek to give richness to critique by forging any critique to sensuousness, to historical reality, and to what exists in possibility.

Dilemmas and Contradictions in Social Theory

The pursuit of historical possibility is the first project of critical social science. And given the fact that the potentialities of a thing or a situation are not given in the appearance of the thing, the onus is on us as social theorists to cultivate a quality of mind which allows us to think about new, alternative futures. In this case, the generalization that patriarchal domination has always existed in the past does not constrain us to accept that it must also be the same way in the future. As Arthur Brittan and Mary Maynard elegantly put it, the fact that it appears to be universalized in all extant societies does not entitle us to read history retrospectively, to give it the status of an inevitable and immutable phenomenon. Its apparent universality today does not mean that this has to be the case in the future.[41]

It is in this context that the Frankfurt School's critique and rejection of positivist social science takes on added importance. The School's point is that it is the style of positivist social science to make sacred the facts that it presents. It describes, and even seems to take pride in not seeking to transcend, what is. By not theorizing what could possibly be, but merely describing what is, such a theory duplicates and eventually lends support to, the status quo, however immoral or repressive that status quo is. Small wonder that Marcuse charges that positivist/technical social science is ideological and 'false,'[42] concerned more with relations between things than with relations between people, placing quantity over quality.

Now, nothing in this discussion is meant to imply a rejection of the relevance of Marxian theory to the understanding of patriarchy. Neither do the critical remarks announce a wholesale renunciation of Marxian insights. Indeed, we feel, with Maureen Mackintosh, that a concept such as the social relations of production, and its importance to an understanding of the division of labor in society, is one of the most useful insights which Marxist economic theory has brought to an understanding of sexual division.[43] The Marxian paradigm has always been a powerful one for understanding society, and there is no doubt that it can continue to be used as a great searchlight on social processes, including the problem of women's oppression. But because traditional Marxism acknowledges the existence of male dominance but does not make that recognition central to its theory or practice, feminists do not see contemporary Marxism as being energetically committed to challenging male dominance. Indeed, they see no reason to believe that Marxist commitment to feminism will be any stronger in the future.[44] We do not necessarily share this pessimism.

Marxism can be used to develop a theoretical framework in which to analyze the problems of women's oppression. The critical point is that the Marxian paradigm, **narrowly interpreted**, may not be sufficient to settle the quandary over the pervasiveness of patriarchy. A critical theory of modern society must seek to go beyond Marx in the key sense of breaking away from any critique whose exclusive form is the traditional critique of political economy. Prompted by the feminist critique of patriarchy, Marxian theory might fruitfully pursue its own unfinished or underdeveloped critique of ideology and mass culture, and inaugurate a Marxism of the everyday cultural practices which promote acquiescence to the patriarchal status quo. This is clearly an important challenge.

It was from Marx that we learned that, as theorists, we must always engage in ceaseless criticism of social processes, if we hope to strip such processes of the 'natural' immediacy and sedimentation in which they appear in everyday consciousness. Only until such time as we use our critical intelligence to reflect on the practice of everyday life will facts such as patriarchal domination, and indeed other patterns of inequality, appear not as natural, but historically specific contrivances. It is still to Marx that we return when we seek to think and act in ways which counteract the possible eclipse of critical reflection. The understanding of the structural subordination of women in society and the perpetuation of capitalist patriarchal relations must be facilitated by a theoretical analysis of patriarchy. Such an analysis, in turn, has to be premised on a critique of ideology as praxis.

We have indicated that ideology, and the tyranny of patriarchal commonsense, obscure and mystify social reality. Over and above the sustained critique of capitalist society, Marxist theory has also bequeathed to social science the need to constantly articulate human possibilities. There is a challenge to build on this. Underlying this chapter is a Promethean idea that humans have the capacity to create the cultural world and realize themselves through labor. This is

Dilemmas and Contradictions in Social Theory

how history is to be sociologically interpreted. To the extent that patriarchy, as a system of power, thwarts this capacity by creating the conditions for alienation, the devaluation of women, reification and ideological sedimentation, a critical social theory which seeks to demystify and **reveal** relations **must** by pursued. What this chapter has attempted to do is to situate the problem of inequality, as experienced by women, in a theoretical context. Change will not come about in the absence of political practice. In the meantime, ceaseless critique, philosophical vision and daily struggle will help to put an urgency in the political program for radical social change.

NOTES

1. Roisin McDonough and Rachel Harrison, "Patriarchy and relations of production," in Annette Kuhn and Ann Marie Wolpe (eds.), **Feminism and Materialism: Women and Modes of Production**, London: Routledge and Kegan Paul, 1978, p. 31; see also Zillah Eisenstein "Developing a theory of capitalist patriarchy and socialist feminism" in Zillah Eisenstein (ed.), **Capitalist Patriarchy and the Case for Socialist Feminism**, New York: Monthly Review Press, 1979, pp. 11, 15; Isaac D. Balbus, **Marxism and Domination: A Neo-Hegelian, Feminist, Psychoanalytic Theory of Sexual, Political, and Technological Liberation**, Princeton, N.J.: Princeton University Press, 1982, pp. 63, 65. For a comprehensive source of materials on this subject, see **Feminism and Women's Issues: An Annotated Bibliography and Research Guide**, compiled by G. Llewellyn Watson, with the assistance of Janet P. MacMillan, 1987, University of Prince Edward Island. This computerized Bibliography contains over 7,000 entries covering various issues having to do with women and feminism in modern society.

2. Friedrich Engels, **The Origin of the Family, Private Property and the State**, New York: International Publishers, 1972, p. 129.

3. See, Heidi Hartmann, "The unhappy marriage of Marxism and Feminism: towards a more progressive union," in Lydia Sargent (ed.), **Women and Revolution: A Discussion of the Unhappy Marriage of Marxism and Feminism**, Montreal: Black Rose Books, 1981, p. 2.

4. Among other works, see Balbus, **op.cit.**, p. 169; Eisenstein, **op.cit.**, p. 17; Heidi Hartmann, "Capitalism, patriarchy and job segregation by sex," **Signs**, Vol. 1, #3, Spring, 1976, p. 38; Veronica Beechey, "On patriarchy," **Feminist Review**, Vol. 3, 1979; Adrienne Rich, **Of Woman Born: Motherhood as Experience and Institution**, New York: W. W. Norton, 1976, pp. 57-58; Linda Phelps, "Patriarchy and Capitalism," **Quest**, vol. 2, #2, Fall, 1975; and Kate Millett, **Sexual Politics**, New York: Avon Books, 1971, p. 25. Millett was, of course, one of the pioneers in utilizing the concept of patriarchy in the

analysis of the structural subordination of women. Her analysis is somewhat flawed, however, by her full-scale rejection of Marxism and class analysis as relevant for understanding women's oppression. Patriarchy was everything that was needed for that explanation. This amounts to throwing out the baby with the bathwater. Marxian theory of domination may be inadequate, if taken alone, to explain all the facets of women's oppression. But the insights which it provides for the structural analysis of capitalist society cannot be ignored if we are to make sense of patriarchy as it manifests itself in contemporary class/capitalist societies. Patriarchy cannot be understood in and of itself, dismembered from class structure, the state and the whole panoply of normative institutions in society, all of which, given the uncritical way in which they work, communicate patriarchy to the consciousness as if it were part of an externally given order that was inevitable and immutable. At least, Marxian social theory attempts first and foremost to grasp things **dialectically**, that is, in terms of structural relationships and historicism. For more, see G. Llewellyn Watson, **Social Theory and Critical Understanding**. Washington, D.C.: University Press of America, Inc., 1982.

5. Eisenstein, **op.cit.**, p. 31; and Eisenstein, "Some notes on the relations of capitalist patriarchy," in Eisenstein, **op.cit.**, p. 48; Hartmann, "The unhappy marriage...," p. 22. See also the important work **Women and the Public Sphere: A Critique of Sociology and Politics**, edited by Janet Siltanen and Michelle Stanworth, London: Hutchinson, 1984. Siltanen and Stanworth argue persuasively that the private women – public man conception misleads as to the relationship of the political to both private and public, and that it fosters misunderstandings of the character and genesis of the political potential of both men and women. They therefore highlight the need to "interrogate more rigorously the theoretical terrain on which the feminist engagement with male-stream writings has taken place, particularly the unreflected emphasis upon the opposition between private women and public man." (pp. 185-208)

6. The discussions of this subject are varied, often rich, and frequently controversial. Some of the better-known are Margaret Benston, **The Political Economy of Women's Liberation** (a New England Free Press pamphlet); Peggy Morton, "Women's work is never done," in **Women Unite** (Toronto: Canadian Women's Educational Press, 1972); Mariarosa dalla Costa, "Women and the subversion of the community" and Selma James, "A woman's place," in **The Power of Women and the Subversion of the Community** (Bristol: Falling Wall Press, 1975); Lise Vogel, "The earthly family," **Radical America** 7 (July-October 1973); Wally Secombe, "The housewife and her labour under Capitalism," **New Left Review** 83 (January-February 1973); B. Magas, H. Wainwright, Maragaret Coulson, "The housewife and her labour under Capitalism - a critique" and Jean Gardiner, "Women's domestic labor," **New Left Review** 89 (January-February 1975); pp. 47-58, and 59-71; Ian Gough and John Harrison, "Unproductive labour and housework again," **Bulletin of the Conference of Socialist Economists**, Vol. 4, no. 1 (1975); Jean Gardiner, Susan Himmelweit and Maureen Mackintosh, "Women's domestic labour," **Bulletin of the Conference of Socialist Economists**, Vol. 4, no. 2 (1975); Wally Secombe, "Domestic labour: reply to critics," **New Left Review**, no. 94 (November-December 1975), pp. 85-96; Terry Fee, "Domestic labor: an analysis of housework and its relation to the production process," **Review of Radical Political Economics**, Vol. 8, no. 1 (Spring 1976), pp. 1-8; Susan Himmelweit and Simon Mohun, "Domestic labour and capital," **Cambridge Journal of Economics**, Vol. 1, no. 1 (March 1977), pp. 15-31; Ira Gerstein, "Domestic work and Capitalism," **Radical America**, Vol. 7, no. 4-5, July-Oct. 1973, pp. 101-128; John Harrison, "Political economy of housework," **Bulletin of the Conference of Socialist Economists**, Vol. 3, no. 1, 1973; Bonnie Fox (ed.), **Hidden in the Household: Women's Domestic Labor Under Capitalism**, Toronto: Women's Press, 1980; Meg Luxton **More Than a Labour of Love: Three Generations of Women's Work in the Home**, Toronto: The Women's Press, 1980.

7. "The housewife and her labor under capitalism"; see, also, Maureen Mackintosh, "Gender and economics: the sexual division of labor and the subordination of women" in Kate Young, **et al.**,

(eds.), **Of Marriage and the Market: Women's Subordination in International Perspective**, London: CSE Books, 1981, pp. 1-15.

8. Janet Sayers, **Biological Politics: Feminist and Anti-Feminist Perspectives**, London: Tavistock, 1982, p. 153.

9. Eisenstein, "Developing a theory...," p. 31. For extensive discussion of how this ideology operates at the formal level of schooling, see Elena Belotti, **Little Girls**, London: Writers and Readers Publishing Cooperative, 1973; Rosemary Deem, **Women and Schooling**, London: Routledge and Kegan Paul, 1978; Rachel Sharp, **Knowledge, Ideology and the Politics of Schooling: Towards a Marxist Analysis of Education**, London: Routledge and Kegan Paul, 1980; and Ann Marie Wolpe, **Some Processes in Sexist Education**, London: Women's Research and Resources Centre, 1977. Michelle Barrett points out that the everyday cultural imagery of gender in our society has been incorporated into the very framework in which we receive and assess all forms of knowledge. See Michelle Barrett, **Women's Oppression Today: Problems in Marxist Feminist Analysis**, London: Vergo, 1980, p. 149.

10. See Adrienne Rich, "Compulsory heterosexuality and lesbian existence," **Signs** 5 (4), 1980, pp. 631-60; Shulamith Firestone, **The Dialectic of Sex: The Case for Feminist Revolution**, New York: Bantam Books, 1970, pp. 1-12; and D.H.J. Morgan, "Women as a social class," in Morgan, **Social Theory and the Family**, London: Routledge and Kegan Paul, 1975. The reader should note, here, the thinly veiled racism which comes to the surface in Firestone's discussion of rape, pp. 108ff.

11. See Patricia Marchak, **Ideological Perspectives on Canada**, Toronto: McGraw-Hill Ryerson, 1982, pp. 1-2. In this connection, see the truly excellent book by Alison Jaggar, **Feminist Politics and Human Nature**, Totowa, N.J.: Rowman and Allanheld, 1983, especially chapter 11: "Feminist politics and epistemology: justifying feminist theory." Jaggar's book is to be considered a major contribution to feminist thought, offering as it does a penetrating discussion of ideology in general and patriarchal ideology in particular.

All told, it provides a thoroughgoing critique of mainstream scholarship from a feminist perspective.

12. See the discussion on this in Watson, **op.cit.** And for some excellent **sociological** accounts of ideology see the following recent works: Nicholas Abercrombie, et al., **The Dominant Ideology Thesis**, London: George Allen and Unwin, 1980; Louis Althusser, **For Marx**, London & New York: Pantheon Books, 1969; Nigel Harris, **Beliefs in Society: The Problem of Ideology**, London: C.A. Watts, 1968; Centre for Contemporary Cultural Studies, **On Ideology**, London: Hutchinson, 1978; Alvin Gouldner, **The Dialectic of Ideology and Technology**, New York: Seabury Press, 1976; Ron Eyerman, "False consciousness and ideology in Marxist theory," **Acta Sociologica**, Vol. 24, #1-2, 1981, pp. 43-56; Jorge Lorrain, **The Concept of Ideology**, London: Hutchinson, 1979; D. Miller, "Ideology and the problem of false consciousness," **Political Studies**, Vol. 20, 1972, pp. 432-47; Colin Sumner, **Reading Ideologies**, New York: Academic Press, 1979; and Rachel Sharp, **op.cit.**

13. Harris, **op.cit.**, pp. 22, 27, 45-46. John Urry has recently suggested that much of what is customarily taken as ideology (in capitalist societies) is properly part of the practices of "civil society." In our view, Urry's very turgid and opaque book, inspite of the title, introduces an unnecessary obscurity to the understanding of capitalist ideology. If he is in fact right about ideology as simply part of the practice of civil society, this makes it all the more mandatory to understand civil society **ideologically.** See his **The Anatomy of Capitalist Societies: The Economy, Civil Society and the State**, London: Macmillan, 1981.

14. Eisenstein, "Developing a theory...," p. 28; and see Veronica Beechey, "Female wage labor in capitalist production," **Capital and Class**, 3, 1977, p. 47. Beechey notes that one of Engels' faults was that he failed to acknowledge that the patriarchal family remains and persists in industrial capitalist society because of its fundamental economic and ideological importance to the capitalist mode of production. This is not, in our view, a simplistic functionalist argument,

but an observation of the complex ways in which patriarchy as ideology **and** relations, and capitalism as ideology **and** relations interpenetrate and cross-fertilize to sustain the structural subordination of women.

15. Stanley Aronowitz, **The Crisis in Historical Materialism: Class, Politics and Culture in Marxist Theory,** New York: Praeger, 1981, p. 62. In reality, capitalist ideology either ignore the facts of the exploitation of women's labor in housework, or else mystifies it to an essential, inevitable aspect of the human condition.

16. Christine Delphy, **The Main Enemy: A Materialist Analysis of Women's Oppression,** London: Women's Research and Resources Centre, 1977; R. Dunbar, "Female liberation as the basis for social revolution," in R. Morgan (ed.), **Sisterhood is Powerful,** New York: Random House, 1970; Mary Daly, **Gyn/Ecology: The Metaethics of Radical Feminism,** Boston: Beacon Press, 1978; Nancy Chodorow, "Family structure and feminine personality," in **Women, Culture and Society,** edited by Michelle Zimbalist Rosaldo and Louise Lamphere, Stanford: Stanford University Press, 1974; and Sherri Ortner, "Is female to male as nature is to culture," in Rosaldo and Lamphere, **op.cit.**, pp. 67-87. This position was, of course, Firestone's early thesis in her **Dialectic of Sex.**

17. Alice Rossi, "A biological perspective on parenting," **Daedalus** 106, #2, Spring, 1977, pp. 1-31.

18. Ortner, **op.cit.**

19. **Ibid.**, pp. 83, 87. See also Elizabeth Janeway, **Man's World, Woman's Place: A Study in Social Mythology,** New York: Delta Books.

20. For further discussion on this theme, see Watson, **op.cit.**, especially chapter 8. The argument must be pursued that we cannot take for granted the assumptions which educators or other influential members of society purvey from day to day in the name of value-free social or scientific inquiry. Knowledge, sociologically understood, is not neutral, but reflects the interests of those who produce it. As Marx was keen to point out, the

development of science is only one aspect of the development of human beings' productive activity. It is impossible to dislodge or amputate it from the social nature of human activity and in particular from the normative quality of social products. See Karl Marx, **The Grundrisse: Introduction to the Critique of Political Economy**, Harmondsworth: Penguin, 1973, pp. 539-41.

21. L. Holliday, **The Violent Sex: Male Psychobiology and the Evolution of Consciousness**, Guerneville, Calif.: Bluestockings Books, 1978, p. 131.

22. Sayers, **op.cit.**, chp. 5. Sayers points out that Simone de Beauvoir is virtually alone among feminists opposed to biological essentialism to give weight to both the biological and the social factors influencing women's experience of motherhood. (p. 167)

23. Eisenstein, "Some notes on ...," p. 44; and see Sayers, **op.cit.**, for a good analysis of this. Monique Couture-Cherkin puts the whole matter this way: "Men make the decisions for us in the economic and social arena, and they also decide about our body ... It is not because we have periods, give birth, breast feed and have abortions that our professional life is blocked! It is blocked because we have accepted a sexual life governed by the power relations between men and women ...[and by] the millions of duties that govern people's lives, done exclusively and freely by women!" See her "Women in Physics," in Hilary and Steven Rose (eds.), **The Radicalization of Science**, London: Macmillan, 1976, pp. 65-75.

24. Hester Eisenstein, **Contemporary Feminist Thought**, Boston: G.K. Hall & Co., 1983, p. 18; and Jaggar, **op.cit.**, p. 221. In this connection see, further, Patricia Linenberger, "What behavior constitutes sexual harassment?" **Labor Law Journal**, vol. 34, #4, April 1983, pp. 238-247; Catharine A. MacKinnon, **Sexual Harassment of Working Women: A Case of Sex Discrimination**, New Haven and London: Yale University Press, 1979; Mary Bularzik, "Sexual harassment at the workplace," **Radical America**, vol. 12, #4, July-Aug. 1978, pp. 25-43; and Dierdre Silverman, "Sexual harassment: working women's dilemma," in **Building Feminist Theory**, New York and London: Longman, 1981 (this article first

appeared in **Quest: A feminist quarterly**, vol. III, #3, Winter, 1976-77) and Elaine Weeks, Jacqueline Boles, Albeno Garbin and John Blount, "The transformation of sexual harassment from a private trouble into a public issue," **Sociological Inquiry**, vol. 56 (4, Fall) 1986, pp. 432-55.

25. For example, Marlene Dixon, **Women in Class Struggle**, San Francisco: Synthesis Publications, 1978. It seems that one of the hottest debates within the feminist movement turns on the question of the part played by capitalism in the origins and perpetuation of women's subordination. It is the question which divides the feminists into radical, socialist, liberal and Marxist camps. For more on this, see C. Nelson and V. Olesen, "Veil of Illusion: a critique of the concept of equality in Western feminist thought," **Catalyst**, 10-11, 1977, pp. 8-36; Lydia Sargent (ed.), **op.cit.** (fn 3 above); Zillah Eisenstein (ed.), **Capitalist Patriarchy...**; and Jaggar, **op.cit.**

26. See, here, Anthony Giddens, **Sociology: A Brief but Critical Introduction**, New York: Harcourt Brace Jovanovich, Inc., 1982, p. 128 ff; Balbus, **op.cit.**, p. 65; and Al Szymanski, **Class Structure: A Critical Perspective**, New York: Praeger, 1983, p. 499. For a good discussion of patriarchy in relation to the family, see Annette Kuhn, "Structures of patriarchy and capital in the family," in Annette Kuhn and Ann Marie Wolpe (eds.), **op.cit.**, pp. 42-67.

27. Maxine Molyneux, "Women in socialist societies: problems of theory and practice" in Kate Young, **et al.**, **Of Marriage and the Market**, op.cit., pp. 167-202; Balbus, **op.cit.**, and see Zillah Eisenstein (ed.), **Capitalist Patriarchy and the Case for Socialist Feminism.**

28. Szymanski, **op.cit.** Along these lines Margaret Stacey and Marion Price have gone out of their way to emphasize that, contrary to the popular image, "women are not equally and universally oppressed and, most importantly, some women oppress other women." While their historical, cross-cultural analysis of women and power is useful for understanding women's position in different societies, it is flawed, in our view, by the scant attention which it pays to the **ideological**

sedementation of patriarchy. See Stacey and Price, **Women, Power and Politics**, London: Tavistock, 1981.

29. See, for instance, Janet Salaff and Judith Merkle, "Women and revolution: the lessons from the Soviet Union and China," **Socialist Review**, 1, (4), 1970, pp. 39-72; Richard Stites, **The Women's Liberation Movement in Russia: Feminism, Nihilism and Bolshevism**, Princeton: Princeton University Press, 1978, pp. 329-41; Alena Heitlinger, **Women and State Socialism: Sex Inequality in the Soviet Union and Czechoslovakia**, London: Macmillan, 1979; Elizabeth Croll, **Feminism and Socialism in China**, London: Routledge & Kegan Paul, 1978; Balbus, **op.cit.**, pp. 62, 74; Aronowitz, **op.cit.**, H. Scott, "Women in Eastern Europe" in J. Lipman-Blumen and J. Barnard (eds.), **Sex Roles & Social Policy**, London: Sage, 1979, p. 221; and Eli Zaretsky, "Capitalism, the family, and personal life" **Socialist Revolution**, 13-14, Jan.-April 1973 and May-June 1973.

30. Balbus, **op.cit.**, p. 73.

31. **Ibid.**, p. 68.

32. Ibid., pp. 77, 79. See also Paul Smith, "Domestic Labor and Marx's theory of value," in Annette Kuhn and Ann Marie Wolpe (eds.), **op.cit.**, pp. 198-219.

33. Aronowitz, **op.cit.**, pp. 4, 66; and cf. Bruce Brown, **Marx, Freud and the Critique of Everyday Life: Toward a Permanent Cultural Revolution**, New York: Monthly Review Press, 1973.

34. Balbus, **op.cit.**, p. 355.

35. For more discussion on the implication of these antinomies see Watson, **op.cit.**, and George Lukacs, **History and Class Consciousness**, Cambridge, Mass.: MIT Press, 1971.

36. See, for example, Nancy Hartsock, "Feminist theory and the development of revolutionary strategy" in Zillah Eisenstein, **op.cit.**, pp. 56-77.

37. For extended discussion on this, see David Held, **Introduction to Critical Theory**, London: Hutchinson, 1980; John B. Thompson and David Held

Dilemmas and Contradictions in Social Theory

(eds.), **Habermas: Critical Debates**, Cambridge, Mass.: The MIT Press, 1982.

38. Balbus, **op.cit.**, p. 61, 355.

39. Nancy Chodorow, **The Reproduction of Mothering**, Berkeley: University of California Press, 1978.

40. Karl Marx, **Capital** (Vol. III), Moscow: Progress Publishers, 1971, p. 817.

41. **Sexism, Racism and Oppression**, London: Blackwell, 1984, p. 215.

42. For the position of the Frankfurt School against positivist social science, see Max Horkheimer, **Critical Theory**, New York: Seabury Press, 1973, especially the seminal essay "Traditional and critical theory," pp. 188-243; Max Horkheimer and Theodor Adorno, **Dialectic of Enlightenment**, New York: Herder and Herder, 1972; The Frankfurt Institute for Social Research, **Aspects of Sociology**, Boston: Beacon Press, 1973; Herbert Marcuse, **One Dimensional Man**, Boston: Beacon Press, 1964, esp. pp. 86-101, 122; Jurgen Habermas, **Knowledge and Human Interests**, Boston: Beacon Press, 1971; **Toward a Rational Society: Student Protest, Science and Politics**, London: Heinemann, 1971.

43. In Kate Young, **op.cit.**, p. 4.

44. Jaggar, **op.cit.**, p. 239.

CHAPTER THREE

POSITIVISM AND THE ROOTS OF CRITICAL THEORY*

I

If one accepts that empirical investigations must terminate in theoretical knowledge, then it is no use pretending that theory can be made easy or that it can be dispensed with. Students in sociology do not always recognize the need for theoretical analysis. Nor do they always identify the connection between one theory and the next.

Understanding theory can be made **easier** by recognizing two important facts: The **first** is that the positivist tradition in sociology reaches back to the Enlightenment's, and later Comte's, hope for a natural 'science of society.' The **second** is that social theory can best be grasped as having two distinct segments:

A. Positivism, with its many assumptions about the nature of science, knowledge, and human beings; and

B. A series of antipositivist schools of meta-theory, including symbolic interactionism, phenomenology, ethnomethodology, critical theory and the sociology of knowledge.

What needs to be grasped (and it renders the task **easier** if it **is** grasped) is that all the perspectives in the second segment, which we usually find in all theory texts, represent, singly or in combination, a gigantic challenge to, and critique of, the assumptions of positivism as developed in Sociology. Functionalism is the best-known of the perspectives building on positivism. I have long argued that one of the great defects of so many 'theory' books in Sociology is that they do not clearly show and discuss the nature of the relationship between positivism and the several and varied schools which raise objections to positivism. To me, this relationship is one of the most important in all of social theory, and what a student of sociology needs to grasp, before theory can be made easier.

Dilemmas and Contradictions in Social Theory

The conventional description given to sociology in North America suggests that we can speak freely of three major paradigms: a conservative one, generally supportive of the status quo (as in Parsonian sociology); a radical one, critical of the existing social order, as exemplified in the works of Marx and Marxists; and a middle-of-the-road, liberal one, typified in the ambivalence and reformist tendencies in Merton's 'middle range' approach. This is a somewhat over-simplified and misleading depiction. In reality the difference between 'conservatives' and 'liberals' is more apparent than real. Both derive from the early positivist development of sociology in North America, as highly uncritical and conservative approaches to the study of society. Both have understood themselves as existing to combat and discredit the radical and politically sensitive ideas of Marx and Marxist sociology.

In a limited sense, the perspectives associated with symbolic interactionism, ethnomethodology and phenomenology can be termed 'liberal' in that they tend often not to explicitly question the social system as a whole, or the structure of power that sustains it. This is one of their major weaknesses. But their claim to legitimacy turns on their challenge to the major assumptions of positivism such as value-neutrality, disinterestedness and objectivity.

II

For present purposes, positivism should be taken to be the view that, in the realm of human knowledge, the natural sciences take pride of place, and provide a model for all other bodies of knowledge. This implies minimally two things: **One**, that other fields of inquiry must emulate the natural science model, if they are to produce genuine knowledge; and **two**, that fields of inquiry where this cannot be done cannot produce real knowledge, or can at best produce knowledge of an inferior kind.[1]

It will be useful, then, to offer next some of the key assumptions of positivism, and very briefly sketch the structural and historical context in which some of its tenets have acquired strong roots in North America. Once these assumptions are revealed, it might become easier to understand why the many anti-positivist

Positivism and the Roots of Critical Theory

schools exist, and exist in such a combative fashion toward positivism.

Some of the key assumptions of positivism are:

1. That phenomena dealt with by social sciences are identical to those of the natural sciences; therefore, the methodology of the natural sciences is appropriate for sociology.

2. That there is one, and only one method for generating knowledge - the scientific method, and that this is a method which produces knowledge superior to that produced by any other method.

3. That knowledge is inherently neutral. Here positivism is not interested in reflecting on the relationship between human interests and styles of theorizing. Rather, there is commitment to the belief that there is a knowable world 'out there' that has a structure and form that can be grasped by the competent investigator who is value-neutral and committed to nothing but the search for truth. This commitment encourages us to believe (falsely, I think) that an objective, external reality is accessible to us without reflection or interpretation - without the implementation of human interests. This must be termed the fallacy of objectivism.

4. That the standard of certainty and exactness in the natural sciences is the only valid explanatory model for scientific knowledge. This is the myth of scientism.

5. That, as a 'science' sociological knowledge has no logically given implications for practical policy or for the pursuit of values. Rather, it is said to be a neutral science whose aim is to provide high level empirical propositions as the basis for accurate prediction and control of social phenomena. It describes what is; but has nothing to say about what **ought** to be.

6. That it is necessary and desirable to carry on analysis in terms of dualities and abstract dichotomies referred to in the previous chapter: science/ideology; fact/value; theory/practice; individual/society; knowledge/human interests; and so on, reminiscent of Kant's famous distinction

Dilemmas and Contradictions in Social Theory

between noumena and phenomena.

The standpoint of the modern-day positivists is often quite dogmatic and anti-philosophical. Papineau, for instance, claims for his book no less than that it is a 'defense of the view that the social sciences can and ought to conform to the standards set by the natural sciences.'[2] Similarly, Babbie claims that 'human social behavior can be subjected to scientific study as legitimately as can atoms, cells and so forth.'[3] These views can be taken to represent a very common, hard-nosed mode toward sociology in general, and sociological methodology in particular. To the degree that sociologists unrepentantly hold to this position, they can potentially exercise a restrictive, conservative influence on the shape of the discipline. Working in certain contexts, such as on the editorial boards of academic journals, these sociologists could effectively dismiss qualitative research without compunction.

This, then, is the foundation on which mainstream sociology in North America is built. Since Comte, positivism has been the most influential theory of knowledge in sociology. And the majority of sociologists today continue to believe that there can be a natural science of society, concerned only with a purely objective search for law-like generalizations. The majority of sociologists today still feel that the coming of age of the discipline depends on becoming more positivistic. In North America, the wish to establish sociology as such a science was always present in a disguised liberalism, although there was a period in the 1920s and 1930s when the Chicago School style of sociology took pride of place. But as the discipline grew increasingly preoccupied with being scientific, and as more scholars outside the Chicago style grew more resentful of Chicago's dominance,[4] positivism via structural functionalism gradually took centre stage, securing its institutional base at the east coast Ivy League Schools in the mid 1930s.

The two decades after World War II were dominated by Talcott Parsons's grand synthesis of Weber, Durkheim, Pareto, Marshall, and subsequently Freud. But not Marx. Parsons's 1937 **The Structure of Social Action**, set new goals and directions in what was the heyday of an expanding field. It was during this period that Parsons, together with a number of eminent colleagues and students developed and consolidated the basis of structural functionalism, lending American and Canadian sociology at least the appearance of an overarching coherence.[5]

But the 1950s, in particular, which saw the elaboration of Parsons' world-view was, politically speaking, a conservative and uncreative period. It was a period characterized above all, especially in the U.S., by the rigid attitudes and relationships of the Cold War, by McCarthyism and the suppression of critical perspectives, by naive ideologies of unlimited economic growth and affluence, by an ideology of developmentalism which said in effect that Americans would inherit the earth. Finally, there was the infamous 'end of ideology' celebration, which, as it turned out was hopelessly premature. What these ideologies expounded was a thesis that, in the West, in the 1950s, there was an exhaustion of political ideas, since we had finally achieved stable democracy and had eliminated the need for critical debate and questioning of the social ends of society.

In short, we had reached a point where ideological conflicts were simply a thing of the past. In Canada, we were experiencing a period of unprecedented economic prosperity piloted by the post-war economic boom. We were in no mood to criticize the system, or question capitalism. All in all, what was being entrenched in this period was a highly conventional social science, with a major emphasis on social order, and a firm commitment to and acceptance of the existing capitalist arrangements. Such a social science became known for studying societal issues in isolation from one another, and from the larger frameworks of such practices as sexual, racial and class oppression.

It is easy to see how the 'end of ideology' ideas fitted into the functionalist scheme being worked out by Parsons and his students, and into the general intellectual atmosphere of this period. Functionalism provided an intellectual framework for celebrating the virtues of American society, and for fighting the evils of totalitarianism: fascism and communism. But it never registered a critical note on the highly discriminatory exploitative, and alienating institutions of American society. In his then famous book **Political Man** (1959), Seymour Lipset argued and enthusiastically proclaimed that the workers in the industrial West had achieved industrial and political citizenship. The fundamental political problems of the industrial revolution had been solved, he claimed; we had essentially reached the end of the search for the good life.

How comforting! Only, the theorists of the day had systematically ignored the structurally-rooted issues of the period: power-relations, the burgeoning collective disaffection in the society, and the on-going movements of protest of all kinds. The anti-war movement, civil-rights movement, feminist movement, the critique of mass university were begging for explanation, and needed to be understood. In its isolated and abstract character the social theory of functionalism/end of ideology proved to be completely out of phase with the new historical forces being unleashed within the American state. All was not well at home. The 'science' which prided itself on prediction, did not predict the wide-spread and deep-rooted social protests of the period. Nor could it **explain** the kinds of social conflicts that were manifested everywhere. There was no sense that the society teetered on the edge of an abyss. To put it more paradoxically, the 'end of ideology' thesis was proclaimed and celebrated on the eve of what turned out to be the most **ideologically**-charged decade of the twentieth century in North America, quintessentially the period of intense class struggle in the U.S. and other capitalist countries. One can only conclude that the liberal theorists announcing Nirvana in the midst of structural chaos had not understood the nature of the society they were studying. Perhaps they did not want to understand it. A dialectical sensibility would at least have suspected that the very system being celebrated was pregnant with struggles and social criticisms, and with possibilities for radical social change.

In effect, functionalist sociologists, unhindered for the most part by any serious intellectual opposition, had spent much time and resources consolidating their position, jealously guarding the graduate curriculum and output, but not providing the encouragement for critical evaluation of society. Fundamentally, their major task was to preside over the apotheosis of positivist sociology in North America. Their particular version of social reality did not go unchallenged, but those who advocated a different path to sociological knowledge, and a different view of modern society were few, and they were largely ignored. Before C. Wright Mills' seminal book **The Sociological**

Positivism and the Roots of Critical Theory

Imagination (1959), one can think of sociologists such as Robert Lynd, Barrington Moore, Jr. and Gunnar Myrdal who openly challenged the orthodoxy.[6]

In the atmosphere of functionalism's dominance there was always, of course, talk of a 'conflict sociology.' This was meant to be a rebuke of, and an alternative to, the functionalist assumptions and inherent weaknesses. But although some important messages of dissatisfaction with functionalism were registered, for example the charge that functionalism was plainly conservative and status quo oriented, and was incapable of dealing with change, the so-called 'conflict theory' was not a particularly constructive assault. It was never anything more than a series of ideas associated with those who used Marxian concepts, or who were otherwise critical of positivism a-la functionalism. Conflict theory was not at all as critical of functionalism as it often appeared to be, and it lacked the structural breadth and depth of a fully Marxian perspective. Although not all who espoused a 'conflict' approach would freely utilize Marxian concepts, it was common, in the standard literature, for reference to be made to all anti-functionalist sociologists as 'radical' and/or 'conflict' sociologists - thus adding to the confusion and lack of distinct intellectual integrity of this perspective.

So confused, and ill-defined, in fact, were the differences between a 'conflict sociology' and structural-functionalism, and so superficially grasped were the deep epistemological differences, that suggestions were constantly offered for their synthesis. There is nothing wrong, of course, with proposing theoretical synthesis; in fact, it is to be encouraged in sociology. But such should only be attempted by first recognizing the dissimilarities, not hiding them or diverting attention away from them. In many ways, the self-proclaimed conflict theorists tried to advance a putatively different perspective by adorning it in functionalist clothing. The result was a warmed-over functionalism. The implicit assumption was that conflict sociology had to be rendered aseptic before it would be accepted by the community of sociologists.

Following Parsons's lead, an 'orthodox consensus' which refused to have any truck with Marxism, was carefully nurtured, couched in the dubious dogma of non-ideological, value-free, 'empirical science.' This consensus was what was given bold expression by the 'end of ideology' theorists. They made it easy for sociologists to ignore genuine large-scale human problems, and to focus instead on safe, inoffensive trivia as research topics. The 'end of ideology' thesis served another latent function, namely, that of discrediting radical political and theoretical perspectives. In the theoretical blarney of the orthodox consensus, Parsons was able to proclaim that Marxism was outmoded and irrelevant, and that class conflict was no longer a significant fact in the contemporary world.

By a sort of cultural osmosis, Canada was part of this ethos. No truly critical sociology was being nourished here; and in any event, we were in no mood to criticize, basking as we were in unprecedented economic prosperity and euphoria of the period. This stance took us through to, and culminated in, Expo '67 and Trudeau-mania, and exceptions to this mood, such as the Front de Liberation du Quebec (F.L.Q.), and later the student rebellion, received unmistakable reaction in social control. There has always been a marked absence in Canada of a sociology with a critical or Marxian thrust, so much so that as late as 1976, S.D. Clark, one of the acknowledged deans of Canadian sociology, was still announcing, with some delight, that Marxism (or critical sociology) is alien to our academic tradition. And, says Clark, he cannot see in the proposed programs of work of the new 'critical' sociologists, a sociology emerging that has meaning in terms of the Canadian experience.[7] Translated, this means quite simply that there is no need for a critical theory of society in Canada. This does not sound any different from the end-of-ideology doxology of seventeen years earlier.

III

Given the dismal failure of positivist sociology to offer structural explanations of the turbulent 1960s, it is understandable that its major premises came under relentless assault as the decade of the 1960s unfolded. Beginning in the mid 1960s, critiques of capitalism slowly began to replace its celebration. A combination of ideas which openly challenged the hegemony of the orthodox consensus came from the New Left, the new

Positivism and the Roots of Critical Theory

Feminism and the countercultural movement. What became known as 'Radical sociology' began to raise serious questions about conventional social science and its alleged neutrality. In reality, the critics argued, conventional social science was in league with corporate capitalism, and provided intellectual justification for the exploitation, domination and oppression of large segments of the population. Indeed, one suspects that if the post-war boom had continued to produce bigger and more commodities and consumption levels, without the resultant contradictions of overproduction, environmental degradation, economic crises and structural unemployment, functionalism would still be the dominant paradigm.

And here we return to the anti-positivist sociologies. Some of these perspectives are 'old,' for example, phenomenology; others of more recent origin, for example, ethnomethodology. And while they project different emphases and establish differing priorities for social science, they all depart from positivism in four essential ways: First, they all encourage a move towards humanistic problems, and towards developing a humanistic sensibility. Second, they seek to develop a more explicit philosophical definition of humans as subjects. That is, a conception of human beings as they have, on their own accord, constructed, and later become ensnared in, their own historical arrangements, social practices and ideational schemes. Third, they all question whether human behavior can be completely described in, or explained by, sets of laws directly similar to those of the physical sciences. Fourth, they all explicitly seek to construct sociology as interpretive understanding. They all recognize, the way positivism does not, that sociology stands in a complex relation to its subject-matter, the observer/researcher being, unavoidably, a member of the social world. As such he/she cannot remove himself/herself from that intersubjective world which is an existential product, created and sustained and changed through the human agent.

Now, of all the sociologies which object to positivist claims, by far the most critical and dialectical, and the one with the most comprehensive program is CRITICAL THEORY.

Critical Theory refers to a series of ideas which emerged in Germany in the 1920s and 1930s by a group of

Dilemmas and Contradictions in Social Theory

scholars collectively known as the Frankfurt School. The most well-known of these scholars were Max Horkheimer, Theodor Adorno, Herbert Marcuse and Erich Fromm. But other, lesser known ones, such as Friedrich Pollock, Walter Benjamin and Franz Neumann, and the Institute's first Director Carl Grunberg, were important within the Institute. Today, Jurgen Habermas stands out as the School's most famous thinker, displaying tremendous theoretical scope and vision. Founded in 1923 under the auspices of the Institute of Social Research at the University of Frankfurt, the scholars in the School were, from the start, committed to a program of interdisciplinary study which they hoped would explain, among other things: the defeat of left-wing working class movements and the subsequent rise of Fascism and Nazism in Europe; and the new forms of domination in contemporary society, varied forms which have turned out to be far more subtle and pervasive than Marx thought possible or envisaged.

Indeed, if there is one consistent and unifying theme in the work of these scholars it is **domination**, more specifically a critique of domination. In addition to being Marxist scholars, many of those associated with the Institute were Jewish. And critical theory was by definition a critique of authority. Not surprisingly, therefore, their existence in Germany became more and more uncomfortable, considering that Nazism was also moving towards its political peak. By 1933, under the aegis of Columbia university, the Institute relocated in New York where most of the members remained until after the war, continuing to produce important works on the nature and implications of capitalist social structures.

All in all, whether working in America or in Germany, their overriding intellectual concern was to reappraise Marxian theory, and eventually **all** social theory in the changed and changing historical circumstances of the twentieth century. They wished for critical theory that it elucidate future possibilities which, if realized, would overcome existing contradictions and enhance the rationality of society. Their program was fully committed to recovering the forgotten experience of reflection, thereby preserving some hope for the future and preserving a moment of cultural critique in their work.[8]

Positivism and the Roots of Critical Theory

To fully appreciate the theoretical richness of critical theory, it is important to note that there are at least 5 and possibly six identifiable theoretical sources contributing to the general perspective of Critical Theory. And Habermas's rendition of theory displays a seemingly unbounded faith in the possibility of a synthesis of these several strands. His aim, in brief, is to formulate a comprehensive alternative to the positivist approach to knowledge and social inquiry, drawing upon and utilizing insights from these many sources. The theoretical sources undergirding his version of critical theory are:

1. Marxian Dialectics
2. Hermeneutics
3. Freudian Psycho-Analysis
4. Phenomenology
5. Linguistic Philosophy

1. **Marxian Dialectics.** Critical theory builds on the legacy of Hegelian-Marxian dialectics, that is, the type of analysis which examines relationships, not only as they appear on the surface, but in terms of the contradictions of the social whole, the structural and historical roots of such contradictions, and the inherent possibilities of any given situation.

The subject-object relationship is a unique element in the Marxian dialectics, as is the idea of 'totality,' that is, placing social events and relationships into a larger historical context than might immediately appear on the surface. As a methodological principle, totality implies grasping the relations of the parts to the whole, the revealed to the hidden. It is, in short, a critical method of analyzing modern society, which seeks for the historical and social medium of human praxis. The fundamental claim of the dialectic is that it gives a unified account of the course of human history which renders it comprehensible to the enquiring intellect. As a method of analysis applied to the modern world, the category of totality points us to the need to understand capitalism at once in its economic, political and social manifestations, and in terms of the relations between these.

2. **Hermeneutics.** Hermeneutics can best be regarded as the science of Interpretation. It is a school of social theory which dates back to the 18th century (Dilthey, Weber, Gadamer) and is held together

55

Dilemmas and Contradictions in Social Theory

by the centrality accorded to the notion of **verstehen** in the study of human conduct, and by the objection to the positivist equation of natural and social phenomena. Hermeneutic philosophy insists that the key to understanding subjective consciousness (which humans have; but inanimate objects do not) is interpretation. By encouraging us to reflect on the relations of theory to history and philosophy, it draws out the dependence of interpretive understanding on the **verstehen** approach. Such understanding is viewed as being achieved through discourse (hence the significance of language as a key medium). For hermeneutic authors, history is interpreted not as the mere elapsing of time but as the understanding that parts of the changes which continually occur have been authored by the participants themselves in the process of social living.

The idea of critical reflection is inseparable from the meaning of theory as an interpretive or hermeneutic process. Any adequate social theory will seek to understand the intersubjective meanings of which social life is constituted. And because the social theorist is unavoidably enmeshed in the social world which she/he seeks to understand, the process of theorizing involves some self-understanding. This is the point which Habermas seeks to underscore in recognizing the hermeneutic/interpretive dimensions of social theory. This view directly counteracts the narrow positivist position which has no room for the interpretive categories of social analysis.

3. Freudian Psycho-Analysis. Some of the insights from Freudian meta-psychology are viewed by Habermas as providing a model for understanding the unhappiness of involuntarily socialized men and women, and their discontent in culture. As Habermas puts it 'psychoanalysis is a science incorporating methodical self-reflection.' If reconstructed, it can be a theory of systematically distorted communication. How does it work as a paradigm?

In psychoanalysis, through a process of dialogue, the participants achieve self-knowledge and self-reflection as forms of therapeutic knowledge. The analyst is guided by his/her commitment to helping the subjects (that is, patients) overcome their suffering and distorted conceptions. Such a commitment clearly enables the analyst to guide, probe and encourage the subjects to historical self-knowledge, the key to emancipation. The psychoanalytic model of self-understanding is appealing to critical theory (at least to Habermas) because it is directed towards freeing the patient from influences that dominate him/her, (such as systematically distorted communication) and subordinating those influences to conscious control, thereby expanding the person's autonomy of action. Its methodological features serve as a clue as to how a critical theory of society could generate communicative competence of those experiencing distortions and domination. The sequence here is thought to be: (undistorted) dialogue → self-reflection → increase in autonomy and self-determination → Emancipatory practice.

4. Phenomenology. To the degree that phenomenology can be said to be concerned with understanding the common everyday meanings and symbols used by people, critical theory is attracted to a phenomenological Marxism which seeks to contribute to a theory of consciousness. As a search for the subjective meaning of experience, phenomenology is viewed favorably as a 'moment' (that is, one of the elements of a complex unity) in the Marxian analysis of the labor process. Indeed, hermeneutics and phenomenology seem as one in accentuating the importance of the everyday beliefs and practices of non-specialists, that is, ordinary citizens who operate with a taken-for-granted set of assumptions in the ongoing constitutions of social activity.

The Marxian ontology of labor yields a sort of phenomenology of men and women, in which they instrumentally produce an objective world which, dialectically, appears alien and tyrannical, not because of its intrinsic objectivity, but because of the very way in which that world was produced - through alienated labor. The phenomenological orientation is necessary in order to strengthen the interpretive reflective competence in the everyday and lay understanding of social life. Implicit in Habermas's blending of phenomenology is the idea that the interpretation of culture and history is well within the competence of ordinary people, who must, however, just transcend the deep-rooted alienation engendered in the popular fashion of the scientization of social life.

5. Linguistic Philosophy. (Ordinary Language Philosophy) This is a school which is seen to converge

Dilemmas and Contradictions in Social Theory

on the study of the everyday world, as opposed to that of the scientist. Associated with the works of J.L. Austin, Wittgenstein and Peter Winch, this little-known school of thought has been of some interest to Habermas who thinks it can possibly be a new foundation for social science, if reconstructed to form a theory of communicative competence, or 'universal pragmatics,' as a precondition for universal human emancipation. This 'pragmatics' amounts to nothing less than a neo-Platonic solution to the problem of systematically distorted communication and technocratic politics associated with the bourgeois State. Winch has observed that the tasks of sociology are philosophical ones, namely understanding that human action is **meaningful** in a way in which events in the natural world are not. But in Habermas's scheme, this same idea takes on special significance.

The situation, according to Habermas, is that coming to know and understand the world is a process of constituting the world through language. All interaction is mediated by ordinary language which makes the interaction and mutual understanding between humans possible. Moreover, our cherished principles such as truth, freedom and justice are inherent in the structure of ordinary language. But in capitalist relations, communication is distorted because of power relations, and because of the predilection for administrative politics, which papers over the contradictions of society. And the main institutions of daily life in these relations constitute a crucial self-reproducing system of power and domination imposed wholesale on all members of society, thus undermining communicative competence. These institutions fragment knowledge, individualize problems and produce **information** and 'dis-information' as just another commodity.

At the level of politics, systems of ideas generated by the political structure are so designed as to **mystify** the political process. Public politics is then not so much concerned with public discourse, as with giving parliamentary floor-shows and personality contests. In the wake of such charades, the ordinary citizen is quite unclear as to exactly what is happening. Public politics is reduced to 'summits' between world leaders: two at a time (Reagan and Mulroney); or more (the 'western' powers). They 'talk' twice for thirty minutes or seventy minutes, and decide our collective fates, or the future of space research,

Positivism and the Roots of Critical Theory

acid rain or free trade. So utterly useless are these summits, that even before they commence, news reporters usually know what will be decided upon by the leaders. In effect, we live in a condition of ideological distortion and mystification. If genuine public discourse could displace administrative fiat, the public sphere would again become meaningful. Public discourse concerning freedom, justice, and the good life, would be in the hands of autonomous subjects who could make intersubjective choices and informed decisions.

With insights from this perspective, critical theory advocates an 'ideal-speech situation,' that is, a form of discourse in which no form of domination or constraints exists. In such a situation (an ideal world), the task of politics would shift from crisis-management to autonomous public discussion of competing norms; this would, in turn, enable citizens to achieve a rational consensus on societal goals.

IV

It is clear that Habermas's aim is to present a grand synthesis of social theories. And to the degree that his main launch pad is positivism, which he criticizes in order to transcend, he develops some veiled sympathy with positivism. More than that, he sees an interdependence between instrumental and communicative experiences, that is, between positivism and critical theory. What he means is that critical theory, in pursuing a path toward emancipatory and socio-political practice, must not ignore the methodological rigor characteristic of positivism. To his synthesis, then, we might reasonably add a sixth ingredient: positivism. Positivism remains a major irritant, because in setting itself up as a model for **all** knowledge, it becomes too restrictive. And besides, it is to be thoroughly criticized for denying its underlying technical interests, and hence the intrinsically normative character of all sciences, including itself. There is further discussion, later, on the ongoing critique of positivism.

For now, what is noteworthy about this synthesis is that the idea of **interpretive understanding** threads its way throughout, clearly an antidote to the naturalistic sociological stance. And this is congruent with

Dilemmas and Contradictions in Social Theory

critical theory's interest in generating critical knowledge as a tool for emancipating men and women from domination about which there is cultivated ignorance. The idea that it is in communicative interaction that men and women achieve an intersubjective understanding of the world and themselves explains why Habermas wishes to ensure (with his new theory of communication) that the language of discourse adequately reflects the actual historical and structural conditions of life.

It is, Habermas thinks, the refinement of the theory of communication which will provide the normative foundation of a critical theory of society. Many kinds of objections and criticisms can legitimately be brought against Habermas's attempt to draw upon these many theoretical sources, some of which were never meant to have any critical intent. The weaknesses inherent in the psychoanalytic model are discussed elsewhere, and need not detain us.[10] Suffice it to say that what we have at the end of this exercise is a perspective on society and social life that is at once sociological, philosophical, and most of all **critical**. To the extent that the synthesis is critical of its constitutive parts, it also transcends the limitations of the individual positions.

Any effort at theoretical synthesis in social theory is to be encouraged, even though no one expects all syntheses to be harmonious. In many ways, however, harmony per se is less important than the overall attempt to formulate thematic continuity in theoretical understanding. In his time, Marx accomplished a noteworthy synthesis of ideas from German philosophy, French socialism and English classical economics to form his penetrating critical social science. Similarly, critical theory projects a commitment to enlightenment by way of critique, and to advocacy toward a more rational society based on undistorted communication. Critical theorists engage in serious social analysis, and let the political chips fall where they will. For many, this is more like moral philosophy - a position to stay clear of. (See the discussion in Chapter 7.)

I have no problem with this. I have long maintained that sociology is nothing if it is not potentially a critique of society; and part of the critique which it formulates has to be moral in the strict sense of containing a philosophical vision not of what society **is**, but what it could **possibly** be.

Positivism and the Roots of Critical Theory

'Science can never provide moral guidelines for action';[11] sociology probably can, but only to the degree that it develops its ideas about society and politics within a framework of value commitment, the way the classical sociologists did. Critical theory, in conceiving of historical possibilities, can demonstrate with factual evidence that the potential for better arrangements and a more rational order already exists in the level of intelligence creativity, and skills in contemporary society.

The program of Critical Theory is therefore predicated upon a dialectical critique of that which currently exists. As a social theory which confronts the real with the possible, critical theory has a transformative intention. Not only must such a theory of society be critical of the social totality; 'it must go beyond the level of the cultural meanings to reveal and criticize the distorted understandings (including positivist science) which derive ultimately from the contradictions inherent in the structure of society itself. Ideological misunderstandings and the societal conditions that make them possible are the twin targets of a critical theory.'[12] These issues will concern us in the next two chapters.

Dilemmas and Contradictions in Social Theory

A SUMMARY TO SITUATE CRITICAL THEORY:
Its relation to other theoretical perspectives;
its own theoretical sources;
and its critical project or program

I	II	III
	CRITICAL THEORY: Theoretical Sources	PROGRAM OF CRITICAL THEORY:
A. Analytical-Empirical Science: Positivism (structural-functionalism)	1. Marxian Dialectics	1. Critique of Positivism
	2. Freudian Psycho-Analysis	2. Critique of Marxism
B. Anti-Positivist Schools of Meta-Theory:	3. Phenomenology	3. Critique of Modern Capitalist Society:
1. Phenomenology	4. Hermeneutics	a. statism
2. Symbolic Interactionism	5. Linguistic Philosophy	b. culture industry
3. Ethnomethodology	?6. Positivism	c. fetishism of commodities
4. Hermeneutics		d. ideology (domination)
5. **Critical Theory**		e. science & technology
6. Sociology of Knowledge		

Positivism and the Roots of Critical Theory

NOTES

* A portion of this chapter was first delivered as a guest lecture at Concordia University in Montreal in January 1986, as "Critical theory and positivism: sociological perspectives in Canada." I am grateful to Professor Julio Tresierra of Concordia's sociology department for the courtesy of the 1986 invitation to deliver the lecture.

1. To arrive at the current definition, assumptions and purpose of positivism in sociology, and to understand the position of its critics, the literature on the subject was extensively reviewed. Among the prominent items are: Anthony Giddens, **Positivism and Sociology**, London: Heinemann, 1976; Anthony Giddens, **New Rules of Sociological Method**, London: Hutchinson, 1976; Anthony Giddens, "Positivism and its critics," in Tom Bottomore and Robert Nisbet (eds.), **A History of Sociological Analysis**, New York: Basic Books, 1978; also in Anthony Giddens, **Studies in Social and Political Theory**, London: Hutchinson, 1977; J. Doug House, "A note on positivism," **The Insurgent Sociologist**, vol. 6, #2, 1976; Richard Flacks and Gerald Turkel, "Radical sociology: the emergence of Neo-Marxism perspectives in U.S. sociology," **Annual Review of Sociology**, vol. 4, 1978; P. Cohen, "Is positivism dead?" **Sociological Review**, vol. 28, 1980, pp. 141-176; Max Horkheimer, **Critical Theory**, New York: Seabury Press, 1972; Ted Benton, **Philosophical Foundations of the Three Sociologies**, London: Routledge & Kegan Paul, 1977; Brian Fay, **Social Theory and Political Practice**, London: George Allen & Unwin, 1978; T. Adorno, et al., **The Positivist Dispute in German Sociology**, London: Heinemann, 1976; Russell Keat, **The Politics of Social Theory: Habermas, Freud and the Critique of Positivism**, London: Routledge and Kegan Paul, 1981; S.C. Brown (ed.), **Philosophical Disputes in the Social Sciences**, Sussex: Harvester Press, 1977, esp. chps. 1, 4-6; Margaret Poloma, **Contemporary Sociological Theory**, London: Macmillan, 1979; Josef Bleicher, **The Hermeneutic Imagination: Outline of a Positive Critique of Scientism and Sociology**, London: Routledge and Kegan Paul, 1982; Peter Halfpenny, **Positivism and Sociology**, London: George Allen & Unwin, 1982; John Sewart, "Critical theory and the critique of conservative

method," **American Sociologist,** vol. 13, 1978, pp. 15-22; John Sewart, "Jurgen Habermas's reconstruction of critical theory," in **Current Perspectives in Social Theory,** vol. 1, Greenwich, Conn.: JAI Press, Inc., 1980; A.J. Lally, "Positivism and its critics," in David Thorns (ed.), **New Directions in Sociology,** New Jersey: Rowman and Littlefield, 1976; Derek Phillips, **Abandoning Method,** 1973, chps. 1 and 2; C.A. Bryant, **Sociology in Action,** London: George Allen & Unwin, 1976, chp. 2; Christopher Bryant, "Positivism reconsidered," **The Sociological Review,** vol. 23, #2 (May), 1975; Werner Pelz, **The Scope of Understanding,** London: Routledge and Kegan Paul, 1974; Michael Buraway, "Introduction: the resurgence of Marxism in American sociology," in **Marxist Inquiries: Studies of Labor, Class, and States,** Chicago: The University of Chicago Press, 1982; Alfred McClung Lee, "Humanist challenge to positivists," **The Insurgent Sociologist,** vol. 6, #1 (fall), 1975, pp. 41-50; Daniel Sabia and Jerald T. Wallulis (eds.), **Critical Theory and Other Critical Perspectives,** Albany: State University of New York Press, 1983; Peter McHugh, "On the failure of positivism," in Jack Douglas (ed.), **Understanding Everyday Life,** London: Routledge and Kegan Paul, 1970; Albrecht Wellmer, "Positivism and critical theory," **Continuum,** vol. 8, 1970; David Papineau, **For Science in the Social Sciences,** London: Macmillan, 1978;

2. David Papineau, **op.cit.**

3. Earl R. Babbie, **The Practice of Social Research** (2nd ed.), Belmont, Calif.: Wadsworth Pub. Co. Inc., 1979, p. 34.

4. See George Ritzer, **Contemporary Sociological Theory,** New York: Alfred A. Knopf, 1983, pp. 49-50.

5. See Michael Burawoy, "Introduction: the resurgence of Marxism in American sociology," in **Marxist Inquiries: Studies of Labor, Class and States** (Supplement to vol. 88, of American Journal of Sociology), Chicago: The Chicago University Press, 1982, p. 51.

6. Indeed, the criticisms, denunciations and outright

Positivism and the Roots of Critical Theory

rejection of Mills' work from mainstream sociologists were particularly harsh and cruel, and by any standard of academic decorum went far beyond constructive criticism to ad hominem attacks. Such viscious attacks and dismissive put-down perhaps revealed more about the ideology of his attackers, than about the quality of Mills' work; and incidentally came not only from the Right, but from other segments of the political spectrum. Among the important works which are available on Mills and his life, see Rick Tilman, **C. Wright Mills, A Native Radical and His American Intellectual Roots**, University Park, Penn.: The Pennsylvania State University Press, 1984; Irving Louis Horowitz, **C. Wright Mills: An American Utopian**, New York: Free Press, 1983; Howard Press, **C. Wright Mills**, Boston: G.K. Hall and Co., 1978; Joseph A. Scimecca, **The Sociological Theory of C. Wright Mills**, Port Washington, N.Y.: Kennikat Press Corp. 1977; and John Eldridge, **C. Wright Mills**, London: Tavistock, 1983.

7. S.D. Clark, **Canadian Society in Historical Perspective**, Toronto: McGraw-Hill Ryerson, 1976, p. 144.

8. For excellent coverage of the Critical Theory perspective, see, for example, John Thompson and David Held (eds.), **Habermas: Critical Debates**, Cambridge, Mass.: MIT Press, 1982; Tom Bottomore, **The Frankfurt School**, London: Tavistock Publications, 1984; David Held, **Introduction to Critical Theory**, Berkeley: University of California Press, 1980; Thomas McCarthy, **The Critical Theory of Jurgen Habermas**, Cambridge, Mass.: MIT Press, 1978; Andrew Arato and Eike Gebhardt (eds.), **The Essential Frankfurt School Reader**, New York: Continuum Pub. Co., 1982; Raymond Geuss, **The Idea of a Critical Theory: Habermas and the Frankfurt School**, Cambridge: Cambridge University Press, 1981; Daniel R. Sabia and Jerald T. Wallulis, **op.cit.**; Paul Connerton (ed.), **Critical Sociology**, Harmondsworth: Penguin Books, 1976; Martin Jay, **The Dialectical Imagination**, Boston: Little, Brown & Co., 1973.

Some excellent articles on the critical paradigm include: John Sewart, "Jurgen Habermas's reconstruction of critical theory," in Scott McNall and Gary Howe (ed.), **Current Perspectives** in **Social Theory** (vol. 1), Greenwood, Conn.: JAI Press, 1980, pp. 323-356; **idem.**, "Critical theory and the critique of conservative method," **The American Sociologist**, vol. 13 (Feb.), 1978, pp. 15-22; P. Scott, "Critical social theory: an introduction and critique," **British Journal of Sociology**, vol. 29, #1, 1978, pp. 1-120; Robert J. Antonio, "The origin, development and contemporary status of critical theory," **The Sociological Quarterly**, vol. 24 (Summer) 1983, pp. 325-351; and **idem.**, "Immanent critique as the core of critical theory: its origins and development in Hegel, Marx, and contemporary thought," **British Journal of Sociology**, vol. 32, 1981, pp. 330-45; Ellsworth R. Fuhrman and William E. Snizek, "From observations on the nature and content of critical theory," **Humboldt Journal of Social Relations**, vol. 7, #1, Fall/Winter, 1979/80, pp. 33-51.

9. For example, Habermas, "A positivistically bisected rationalism," in Theodor Adorno, et al., **The Positivist Dispute in German Sociology**, London: Heinemann, 1976, p. 221.

10. See G. Llewellyn Watson, **Social Theory and Critical Understanding**, Washington, D.C.: University Press of America, Inc., 1982, chp. 2.

11. Peter Berger and Hansfried Kellner, **Sociology Reinterpreted: An Essay on Method and Vocation**, New York: Anchor Books, 1981, p. 12.

12. Christopher Lloyd (ed.), **Social Theory and Political Practice**, Oxford: Clarendon Press, 1983, p. 15.

CHAPTER FOUR

THE CRITICAL PROJECT

I

As with Marx, who really launched the critical project, and who through dialectical analysis was able to expose the basic contradictions inherent in capitalist relations of production, contemporary critical theory seeks to understand the fabric of social life as a whole, and in terms of its contradictory forces. The basic presupposition of this approach is that there should be a continual effort to realize Reason as the capacity of thought to understand the existing social reality, to criticize it, and to project alternatives. Such would require a social and political milieu in which men and women, armed with a comprehension of that which is, determined their own futures in a rational and autonomous way, and with a full consciousness of their capabilities and limitations as human beings.

The Critical School has many misgivings about modern society and contemporary theories of such a society. There is the feeling that, the technological consciousness which has come to dominate our period - the Atari mentality - blocks off the type of critical reflection needed to comprehend modern society. It will be seen then in the following discussion that Critical Theory has some serious arguments with whatever short-circuits our attempts to comprehend the social questions of our time.

The positivist approach to the social and cultural world is strongly challenged, so are many of the unquestioned priorities of the capitalist structure. The aim of the overall project is to restore to the idea of social theory the meaning it once had, namely, a critical reflection upon society. Accordingly, the core of the Frankfurt School's program consists of:

1. A critique of positivism
2. A critique of Marxism
3. A critique of modern capitalist society.

Dilemmas and Contradictions in Social Theory

Let us proceed to examine this program in depth.

1. The Critique of Positivism

From the outset, the Frankfurt theorists insisted that critical theory could not be conceived on the model of natural science, because a social theory modelled on natural sciences will be a **technical** science, and hence inherently manipulative. In the case of social science, the objects of manipulation will be people. Methodologically, they question the naturalist orientation dominant in contemporary social science. The interest of critical theory is in self-reflection, in developing alternative stances appropriate to both the subject matter and goals of critical social inquiry, goals which could conceivably lead to emancipation from unrecognized dependencies, and from historically specific forms of constraints on human freedom.

The Frankfurt School's critique of positivism has been a sustained one, from Horkheimer in the 1930s to Habermas in the 1980s. In the 1940s Marcuse, in **Reason and Revolution,** argued quite forcefully that positive philosophy, in contrast to dialectical social theory, tended to equate the study of society with the study of nature; just as Horkheimer had earlier accused positivism of conceiving of the world only as immediately given rather than in terms of what it could possibly be. It established unnecessary dualities which treat human beings one-sidedly, and fragment thought. The fragmentation of thought cannot be the basis for an understanding of the nature of the **social totality.**

For his part, Habermas doubts whether social science may proceed, just as indifferently towards its object of study as natural science apparently does towards its subject-matter. In several of his works, Habermas argues that positivism, by eliminating the activity of self-reflection, has introduced an illusion of pure knowledge which, contrary to positivist claims, is **not** the pure and disinterested product of 'neutral' scientists.[1] One has to reject or drastically modify the methods of the natural sciences in order to analyze cultural products.

The Critical Project

When analyzing social life, a particular kind of understanding is required, if for no other reason than because the object of knowledge also involves the subject. The School attempts to show that the brute 'objective' facts that provide the raw material for the positivist's production of knowledge simply do not exist in the same manner in the social world. Indeed, at every crucial stage in social inquiry, the sociologist faces problems quite unlike those faced by the natural scientist. And by mimicking the objectivity of the natural sciences, we are guilty of a grave error - an epistemological mistake.

If we cannot agree on the fundamental ontological difference between natural and social sciences, perhaps we are never going to agree on alternative ways of **doing** sociology. Like all bodies of knowledge, positivist science is linked to interests. Therefore, one of the aims of the Frankfurt theorists is to thoroughly criticize the positivist claim that facts and value choices are totally separate, and their willingness to attend only to what is **given**. This is a major contradiction in social science. Those sociologists who still wish the facts to 'speak for themselves,' **mis**understand the social nature of 'social facts,' and also evade the critical human task of interpreting social life.

The problem of ethics, or the problem of values or ideology, cannot be conveniently avoided by appealing to scientific facts. Indeed, in social theory, values may be just as fundamental as facts and maybe sociology would be better served if we devoted as much energy to the study of values, as we do to the facts. Both are bound together in an indissoluble dialectical union; both exist in the same universe of discourse and meaning. Since Popper's well-known polemic against some positivists, it should have become commonplace that uninterpreted facts are **meaningless**. And the interpretive process is fundamentally shaped by our value commitment. As Popper himself says: 'Facts as such have no meaning; they gain it only through our decisions.'[2] The decision to impose meaning is the decision to interpret, and that interpretation is, in all systematic inquiry, dependent upon the values we hold. Thus, science can set limits as to what we can and cannot do; it does not, however, free us from the human task of making moral and value choices.

Unwittingly or not, then, to accept uncritically

Dilemmas and Contradictions in Social Theory

the so-called facts as they are given, is to sanction the present social order, to obstruct new visions, and to encourage political quietism. From the point of view of critical theory, sociologists must refuse to regard the established structures and social arrangements, and the ideas that legitimate them (however rigid they may seem), as exhaustive of historical possibilities.

It is understandable, not to say forgiveable, why positivism **reifies**. For in the haste to transform the particular into some purported general or universal 'law,' it confuses the conventional with the natural, the historically contingent with the eternal. The political implications of this are obvious. A reified consciousness reinforces people's acceptance of the status quo or that which currently exists. Instead of providing them with an analysis of their social and historical situation, it reinforces a belief that things must be as they are. This is useful to the dominant ideologies which typically claim for specific forms of consciousness and beliefs that they are somehow natural, universal and perhaps even eternal. Change does not stem from such forms of consciousness.

If one believes that social arrangements are immutable, one is harboring an inherently conservative position, subscribing to what Gouldner called the 'metaphysical pathos,'[3] that is, accepting and accommodating to the presumed inevitability of organizational domination. The absence of an analysis of a social situation means that there is no historical basis for challenging the existing system, let alone changing it. Thus, as Gouldner noted, instead of telling men and women how bureaucracy might be mitigated, many social scientists insist that it is inevitable. 'Instead of assuming responsibilities and striving to further democratic principles wherever they can, many have become morticians, all too eager to bury men's hopes.'[4]

Positivism presupposes a particular (flawed) ontology of men and women. It supposes that individuals are fixed objects in nature, and that this fixity somehow guarantees 'behavioral' regularities and predictable responses amenable to some general law. Positivist sociologists still search for these laws of human behavior. This physicalist theoretical position clearly introduces an a-historical element into social explanations if contingent relationships are mistaken for eternal laws.

We will never arrive at genuine laws comparable to those in nature, precisely because of the ontological character of human beings, and the social and cultural world they produce. Social life is constituted of the intentional actions of men and women. They still have the capacity to change and transform themselves and their world. In doing so, they make history. The historicity of humans and society dictates that social science methodology and explanations will be qualitatively different from the type found in the physical sciences.

In sum, the positivist assumptions of the unity of science, of phenomenalism or objectivism, of value-freedom, of scientism, of reductionism, and of false antinomies, are all strongly challenged, and an alternative model of social inquiry which does logical and historical justice to the constitution of human society, formulated. As we shall discover, the Frankfurt School's critique of positivism is but a small part of their overall theoretical project.

II

2. The Critique of Marxism

The Frankfurt School's critique of Marxism is of the most constructive kind. While they build on Marx and Hegel and agree on the significance of Marx's critique of liberal capitalism, they recognize the need for Marxian theory to be reappraised in the new circumstances of contemporary (late capitalist) society.

In particular, they find it imperative to continually reconstruct and revitalize Marxism to take more fully into account such developmental tendencies in advanced capitalism as increased State intervention, and the transformation of science and technology into a leading productive force and as a sophisticated form of domination. Finally, they have serious questions concerning the role of modern-day working class, and they also see the need to develop a full-fledged critique of culture, a theme which Marx had not fully explored because of his emphasis on a critique of political economy.

Dilemmas and Contradictions in Social Theory

The Frankfurt theorists recognize that Marx and Engels grounded their critical theory in the situation of the proletariat. But in this period of capitalism, there is no full-fledged conscious class equivalent to the working class of the twentieth century. In fact, the working class of the 19th century has been assimilated and pacified, not only through high mass consumption and commodity fetishism, but the rationalized process of production itself. As Habermas puts it,[5] 'the proletariat as proletariat, has been dissolved and rendered socially impotent, for while the mass of the population is proletarian in terms of its role in the process of production, this situation is such that class antagonisms because unresolved, yet suppressed, is no longer conceived as important features of the modern western societies.' The critique of Marxism therefore extends to a disbelief in, and a distancing from, the proletariat as some sort of self-conscious, historically-grounded subjects, who might actively intervene in the process of social transformation in the mature capitalist societies. History has not confirmed the world-historical role of the proletariat in such societies, even with the ongoing protracted crises which have come to characterize late capitalist societies.

Capitalism is still prone to structural crises. That much is immediately evident in the contemporary capitalist societies. But it has done well to integrate the interests of the dominant class with the consciousness of the working class. It is this forged identity of interests which has created a stabilization of capitalism, and ensured its reproduction where Marx thought it might atrophy. Instead of the proletariat within modern capitalism overthrowing the capitalist system, capitalism has served to de-skill these same workers and to undermine worker solidarity in the peripheral Third World regions. Either way, the maturation and sophistication of modern capitalism have served to diminish the potentially revolutionary role of the working class.

Let us extend this discussion to include the following important notes. Orthodox Marxists strongly object to the idea that the proletariat as a world-historical agency is no longer taken seriously by cultural Marxists. They point to the experiences of 'proletarian revolutions' in Vietnam, Cuba, Yugoslavia and Russia - what they term Marxist-Leninist revolutions of the twentieth century - as proof that

The Critical Project

the proletariat is very much a world revolutionary force. These Marxists therefore interpret the modern disbelief in the proletariat as another example of Western academics' negative, anti-Soviet, anti-Socialist ideology. Two important comments are appropriate here.

First, the idea that Marxism can explain every situation of oppression or exploitation, and hence every situation of popular revolt, is unnecessarily dogmatic. No theory can ever explain everything; and that problem is worsened when such a theory is not reconstructed or revised to take into account the changing circumstances of history. It is dogmatic of any theoretical system if it holds that a previously reached conclusion is valid, independently of the objective conditions existing at a given time, and independently of a concrete analysis of such conditions. And Marx, I think, would be critical of those who slavishly cling to the original ideas and views of their masters, overlooking the historical changes that have taken place since these ideas were developed.

There is no question that Marxism, as social theory, offers an inspiring vision, incisive analysis, and an appealing political practice. But to go on to insist that there is no difference between the industrial workers in the factories of New Jersey or Illinois or Quebec, and the sugar workers who helped to make the Cuban revolution, is really to try to torture the truth out of history by absolutist methods. In the U.S.A. and Canada, one can find beach towels made in Poland; winter gloves made in China or Romania, sardines from East Germany, and gherkins and hiking boots from Yugoslavia; and any number of other commodities from socialist countries. The key question in all this then is: 'what does this mean for world proletariat revolution?' The working people who toil in the capitalist factories might wish to change, through revolt, their alienated conditions of work. Does this also hold true for the socialist factory worker? Must we assume that the workers in Romania who produce these gloves for the Western market are as alienated as their western counterparts? If not, are we to expect them to be part of a world revolutionary revolt?

The **second** comment is this. The pessimism and despair which the Frankfurt theorists displayed on the question of class consciousness was not without empirical and historical basis. They could still, if they wished, guard the hope that the future socialist society would be ushered in by the industrial workers of the world, and hold to the naive optimism in the power of 'class consciousness' to change social reality. But for them, the possibility of the proletariat in the West contributing to an emancipatory practice had to be balanced against two key realities. First, the experience of the catastrophic defeat of the working classes in Germany, Italy, and Hungary after the First World War, and the subsequent rise of fascist domination. And second, the apathy, acquiescence and co-optation of workers in the North American arena of emetic consumerism.

Such realities called for a rethinking of Marxism. Already in the early 1920s the 'cultural Marxists', Karl Korsch, Georg Lukacs and Antonio Gramsci, were beginning to suspect that capitalist hegemonic ideology was an important factor occluding working class, revolutionary consciousness. Just how such ideology worked, and how it might be transcended, became a major theoretical preoccupation of the first generation of Frankfurt theorists. They realized, in short, that theories must change in response to changing historical conditions and with the unfolding of new historical realities. A social theory may be quite capable of explaining social change, and yet itself is changing.

A central tenet of Marxism is the link between theory and practice. And this implies, at the very least, that social theories - and particularly Marxism itself - must undergo constant reconstruction to explain more adequately on-going historical changes. Indeed, a basic criterion for assessing the scientific claims of a particular social theory must be its ability or failure to submit to a constant critical evaluation and re-evaluation of its own fundamental principles and assumptions.[6] Marxism cannot be its own exception, and any suppression of careful, critical self reflection amounts to an ideological closure and universal certaintly which are antithetical to genuine Marxism.

If, in the hands of the Frankfurt School, Marxism has lost its practical ally and political heart - a conscious working class with 'radical chains' - then it is not necessarily a matter which can be understood by looking further and further afield for examples to fit

The Critical Project

the original Marxian model. Rather, what is revealed is that capitalist domination and ideological hegemony have turned out to be far more destructive of workers' consciousness than Marx visualized. Of necessity, this calls for a critical analysis of those aspects of capitalist societies which served the double function of pacifying the masses in capitalist societies, and at the same time creating the conditions for the societies' own reproduction. This is the objective of the critical project - an analysis of certain features of modern capitalism as they actually operate from day to day. The point is to comprehend the social arrangements that define, contain, and displace the crises tendencies and contradictions within contemporary capitalism.

We still do not know what sort of objective conditions move people to political action and change. And the question of: 'under what conditions will humans seek to overcome their situation of domination' has not been fully addressed by critical theory, let alone orthodox theory. Nor is the question of **who** will be the self-conscious agents of change been consistently and seriously looked at. In the heady days of the 1960's Habermas had confidence in students, whom he thought enjoyed relative autonomy from the vagaries and destructive anxiety of the capitalist marketplace. Similarly, Marcuse had high hopes that Blacks, or Third World people, or young people and students, would serve as the new revolutionary subjects to replace the industrial proletariat. None of these groups worked out as these theorists thought they might. Habermas's new communication theory identifies no clearly defined group which, given objective indicators of human suffering, could serve as the potential agents for social transformation. We still do not know what it is that will move people to seek to overcome repressive social conditions in capitalist societies. In these societies, even the much better educated and sophisticated workers of the post-World War II period have shown no greater predilection or potential for engaging in critique and struggle that could possibly lead to a radical transformation of material conditions. The nature of intellectual criticism, theoretical understanding, and change, are all deeply problematic in advanced capitalist societies.

Neo-Marxists have not been able to settle the question of who should or could be the radical,

Dilemmas and Contradictions in Social Theory

liberating agents in modern society. In his ambivalent works, Gouldner is lead into the thinking that 'intellectuals' can perform that role because they possess what he calls a 'culture of critical discourse,' and are the progressive force in modern society.[7]

One can only suggest that Gouldner is misguided. His idea that it is intellectuals who, by their professionalism and reason will liberate society, is particularly flawed because his definition of intellectuals includes some of the traditionally more reactionary and conservative elements in modern society. His definition includes bureaucrats, lawyers, specialists in management and industrial organizations and, oddly enough, media elites, whom he thinks are relatively autonomous from other elites, and have a predilection for objective, balanced coverage of news and protest movements. The empirical evidence on the media in industrial societies fiercely contradicts Gouldner's 'faith' in those who 'process' the news and other media events. It is astonishing how someone of Gouldner's stature could have arrived[8] at such a conclusion, given the available evidence.

As John Sewart has noted, Gouldner overemphasizes the nature and potential of his 'new' intellectual class. For the armies of technicians necessary to the postindustrial economy have been educated in business and trade schools where the technocratic world view exists in its strongest form, that is, a world which enthrones questions of means or **techne** and has no need for questions of ends or **telos**.[9] The optimism and trust in the new class of intellectuals is further weakened because Gouldner does not provide the evidence to show that this new class has ever challenged the logic of private capital accumulation, economic efficiency and profit maximization. In our view, the people who would constitute such a class are not part of the solution; they are part of the problem. Sewart rightly asks: 'what has the highly skilled MBA or corporate lawyer been trained to do? Challenge the power of the bourgeoisie or accumulate private capital in the most efficient manner possible?'[10]

In fact, then, Gouldner's 'New Class' is simply the avant garde of the latest version of those (mostly men) who wish to move toward the apotheosis of technical, abstract, mystifying and so-called 'rational' procedures which mask a form of extreme irrationality

The Critical Project

and illogic. Being technology minded, corporate minded and overwhelmingly on the side of the propertied class, they collectively are apostles of growth, all too eager to put absolute faith in technical knowledge as that which will maximize their private aggrandizement. Their so-called 'critical discourse' is a language that omits persons and feelings, that is totally drained of emotion and moral implications. They are the type who populate the modern bureaucratic organization, who, by supplying us with **information overload** overwhelms our capacity to analyze. Theirs is really pseudo-communication. The New Class triumphs by utilizing the electronic media to carry the consumer imagery into every facet of people's lives in the capitalist societies, and **information,** not analysis, not knowledge, is their idiom and source of ego gratification. It is for this reason that universities and other institutions focusing on technological studies do not want their students to ask moral questions. These types of institutions are not the places where we are likely to find faculty who would encourage a commitment to moral issues.

III

3. The Critique of Modern Capitalist Society

The critique of modern capitalist society is a multifaceted one. Again, the major point of the Frankfurt theorists is that, as a social system, modern capitalism has become so firmly established and has developed effective systems of domination to the point where it seems unchallengeable. But it appears that way only because we have not employed critical reflection and structural analysis in our theoretical exercise.

Certain structural features of capitalism, they argue, can be seen to force, manipulate, blind or fool people into ensuring its reproduction and continuation. Working together, these features sustain a thoughtless conformity to, and acceptance of, the status quo, promoting acquiescence, affirmation, and even a fatalistic attitude to existing society. The workings of these elements in contemporary capitalism integrate and stabilize the capitalist mode of production, and in the end succeed in creating an emasculated working class and a general deadening of critical awareness.

Dilemmas and Contradictions in Social Theory

At the end of this process, both individuality and democratic principles are crushed. Singled out for critical analysis, then, are:

(a) statism
(b) the culture industry
(c) the fetishism of commodities
(d) the dominant ideology of capitalism
(e) science and technology

(a) **Statism**

A significant development within modern capitalism which has served to stabilize and manage its structural contradictions and crises, is Statism (or State intervention). Such intervention has increased quite dramatically since the First World War, and it has served to contain and displace the periodic crises - usually a displacement from the economic sphere to the political. Furthermore, the State mystifies the political **meaning** of the crises. What is to be recognized, the critical theorists argue, is that one of the real functions which the capitalist State performs is to provide conditions favorable to the accumulation of **private** capital, and the maintenance of law and order. The stabilizing in itself might very well enable the sufferring caused by such experiences as unemployment to be less severe than it might otherwise be. But what is being preserved is a questionable status quo. On the other hand, as we shall see, the capitalist State is the paragon of inconsistency.

The contradictions which the State manages with its so-called economic programming are permanent features of the liberal democracies, and well known in Canada. They reveal themselves through deficit financing, incomes policy, wage freezing, and the State subsidizing of big business (that is, pork-barrel projects farmed out and tax benefits granted to private industries). Underlying these projects is the State pre-supposition that what is good for private enterprise, is good for the entire society. But the ordinary citizen has no idea of how the entire process is supposed to work to make for a more rational social order. Without such an understanding, there is clearly not much point in advocating radical changes. The contradictions between the interests of the working class and those of the dominant class must be examined rather more closely. These contradictions are ideologically produced; that is, as one ideology produced in one realm of social reality (for example the economic) contradicts the ideology in another realm (for example the cultural) the State intervenes, not to formulate a new ideology, but to further legitimize and stabilize what is in effect a system shot through with contradictions. What contradictions? Let us explore some common ones.

Much of the palaver in which the officials of the State engage does not make sense, nor add up. They invent new catch phrases to, presumably, convey to the population how serious and efficient they are: phrases such as 'job-creation,' 'the private sector,' 'deficit-reduction.' Added to this, the politicians seem to have unbounded faith in the private sector's ability and willingness to do the job-creation, and to generally operate with the larger societal interests in mind. Unfortunately, this is never the case.

It is not understandable how the **contradictions** built into this approach can be downplayed with such ease. In a single week, for instance, (March 1986) two developments occurred which can illustrate this point. The government of Canada announces cost-cutting measures within the Federal civil service to the tune of several billion dollars. Deficit-reduction? perhaps. Job-creation? doubtful. In another sector, the well-loved 'private sector,' General Motors of Canada announced a $2 billion **expansion** to its Oshawa operation. But it immediately makes it clear that the huge expansion would create no new jobs, only secure existing ones, because the expansion would be facilitated through technology,[11] more specifically, through robotization. For this, the world's largest auto maker, the whole point of the robotic assembly-line was to counter falling profits. In 1986, and continuing through into 1987, plant closures and the loss of thousands of jobs have become common features of his gigantic private sector industry. What reasons have we to place total confidence in the private sector for creating the meaningful jobs people desire? For General Motors, the expansion would definitely yield an increased rate of profits; for the unemployed, certainly not a job, new or old. Clearly, it is a miserable myth that 'what's good for GM is good for all of Canada.'

It is very easy to be misunderstood on this. No one who has ever seen, worked on, or even seriously

Dilemmas and Contradictions in Social Theory

contemplated assembly-line work, can believe that it is fulfilling or enjoyable work. It is mindless, boring and alienating work. Yet in the 1930's it was instituted as the answer to unemployment and to mass-production. The mass-production was for greater efficiency, technical rationality-for-profits. In the 1980's, the answer to greater efficiency is not to humanize the work process. To keep ahead of the competition, (to keep surplus profits high, in other words) people become very dispensable, and they in turn see the whole thing as the unstoppable wheel of progress.

In another situation related to GM a few weeks earlier, more contradictions can be illustrated. The Canadian-Israel Committee had voiced opposition to a proposal (before the Canadian Cabinet) by a West German conglomerate to build an arms plant on Cape Breton Island in Nova Scotia to export tanks and armored vehicles to Arab nations. Naturally, the C-I Committee feared that the sale of Canadian-made arms to Saudi Arabia or other Arab nations would escalate the Middle East arms race and would be detrimental to Israel's security. General Motors was also worried about the arms proposal, **but for entirely different reasons.** The problem for GM was that they were already selling armored vehicles to Saudi Arabia from one of their Ontario plants. Consequently, said one official, there isn't enough room for two competing manufacturers in Canada; such a competition would cut into GM's level of profits. What is good for GM is good for private profits, pure and simple.

Consider yet the common contradiction whereby in order for capitalist 'investors' to keep up their level of profits, they reduce one of their costs of production by opting for technical innovation. This means laying off workers, who require paid vacations, sick leaves, maternity benefits and so on. Machines and robots do not! On the one hand, the State 'intervenes' by continually expending billions of dollars on high technology, which is capital-intensive. On the other hand, it doles out huge welfare subsidies for the unemployed.

Consider, also, one other contradiction. Canada has harsh winters; yet the major proportion of the winter gear we need to cope with these winters are **not** made in Canada, but in Korea, Hong Kong, China, Japan, the Philippines. Never mind that many people never wondered why, and perhaps care even less; one must still search for the **meaning** of this. Is it that we do not have the know-how to do the job? This is clearly ridiculous. Is it that we do not have the unemployed labor-pool to do the job? Clearly not. If it is a case that all we wish for is to utilize the 'cheaper' labor overseas we are then into the business of exploiting foreign labor at the expense of unemployment at home.

Small wonder that we face the cultural frustration of commodities that do not fit; that do not last; that do not work. However, we can achieve no understanding of the underlying structures, because the lexicon of the capitalist market situation belies the reality of the marketplace, and distinctly ideological concepts give the structures an appearance of what they are not. The concept of 'value of labor,' for instance, is an ideological concept, that is, a **belief** that a certain quantity of labor power which is expended and paid for in 'wages' represents a 'fair exchange' of equivalents. But this conception effectively conceals the alienation of the worker, and mystifies one of the sources of capitalist profit. Similarly, phrases such as the 'profit motive' is no more than a euphemism for greed; 'competition' a euphemism for cheating; and 'what the market will bear' a euphemism for overcharging.

The profit motive is doubtless one of the root causes of the outpouring of shoddy and unreliable commodities, from clothes to household gadgets to automobile parts. Seeking out the cheapest human labor does not in this context translate into efficient, reliable commodities. In the modern industrial mass production and mass marketing, quality suffers because the key social relationship is money relationship, not one between producer and consumer. We wonder, then, to what extent the foreign worker can be expected to care about products to be used by strangers.

There is a fundamental contradiction between production-for-profit in capitalism, and consumption. The use of labor in an alien, or let us say in a region peripheral to the metropolis, simply because it is cheaper, and therefore able to keep the level of corporate profits rising, has a built-in immorality, where this means ignoring the surplus of unused domestic labor. If we are interested in knowing how a capitalist economy works, we have to bring such contradictions under close scrutiny. Finance ministers

Dilemmas and Contradictions in Social Theory

and the captains of industry do not give us the 'logic' or 'illogic' of the process of capital accumulation. More often than not, their form of communication produces a system of reciprocal misunderstanding.

Paradoxically, as Habermas has shown,[12] the more the modern State involves itself in sophisticated and successful ways in regulating our lives, the more it faces a series of crises: **first,** a **rationality/economic crisis.** This arises because the State has to constantly borrow to fulfill its functions, and thus creates a lasting inflation and financial crisis. Furthermore, because the State is committed to exponential growth and private accumulation, it deems it necessary to occasionally intervene in the so-called free market to ensure that this growth is crisis-free. According to Habermas, this tends to threaten the very existence of the capitalist mode of production, for this same State intervention is expensive. It uses up an increasing amount of revenue, which endangers the necessary process of accumulation and growth.[13] Greater State intervention expands its own bureaucratic apparatus as well. This, in turn, calls for additional revenue. The revenue can be raised through fiscal policies, but the State will imperil itself if it imposes taxation in such a way as to impede the accumulation process as such or to shortcircuit economic growth. It is the attempt to carry out these balancing acts which has created the economic and rationality crises in all the capitalist democracies. It is a 'rationality' crisis because the problems are rooted in the inability of the State to reconcile the different and conflicting interests of private capital.

Second, this same crisis appears in the political arena as a **legitimation crisis:** The underlying cause of the legitimation crisis is the contradiction between class interests. This is due to the fact that the State must secure the loyalty of one class while systematically acting in the interests of another. As the State's activity expands and its role in controlling social reality becomes more transparent, there is a greater danger that this asymmetrical relation will be exposed. Such an exposure would only increase the demands on the resources of the system for further allocations and participation. Such demands the State can ignore only at its peril. On the other hand, the State might act 'tough' by further demonstrating its non-democratic nature, and thus undermining its ideologically founded legitimation system.[14] The contradictions of the capitalist State tightens. If the State cannot find the right strategies to reconcile the conflicting interests that it tries to handle, then it loses legitimacy in the eyes of the population.

Third, a **motivation crisis** comes about when the heavy-hand of the State, together with its inability to solve the deep structural crises, undermine people's motivations for participating in the system at all. This crisis amounts to a malignant public cynicism whereby the electorate or the voting public entertain serious reservations about the credibility and competence of political functionaries. Accordingly, people are seen to be more concerned with what they can gain from the current arrangements, not how they might participate in the democratic process to improve its performance.

Akin to this cynicism is what Therborn has called 'political marginalization' of large sectors of the population in contemporary advanced capitalist societies. As he observed, 'the United States, in particular, has produced an extraordinarily wide degree of marginalization, to the point where only half of the population votes in presidential elections, and much fewer in other elections. Marginalization seems often to be accompanied by a cynically critical view of the rulers.'[15]

The capitalist State, like the State in any other political system, has in its repertoire repressive powers which it can use, and in recent years has deployed at will, to ensure conformity to the dominant ideology. In a democratic society, this is not the most popular option, but in some of the capitalist democracies, as Young **et al** have argued, much contemporary labor legislation is not only aimed at socializing labor to get it to 'agree' to continue production, but also at criminalizing those (for example, pickets) who refuse to be so socialized.[16] This is as true for Britain as it is for Canada and other late capitalist societies. It is social control through State/capitalist domination. It says something, also, about class struggle, where the one working class institution within capitalism which promises to become universal or at least to create worker solidarity - the trade union - comes under such insensitive, legalistic control by the State.

Dilemmas and Contradictions in Social Theory

The complex relationship between the capitalist State, ideology, and the dominant class must be theoretically given as follows. The State governs the subordinate class which provides labor for the dominant class. To facilitate the profit-making, and to ensure a smooth-functioning economic and social infrastructure for the operation of the corporate economy, the State regulates the subordinate class through anti-strike legislation, injunctions, and the repression of trade union activities at the workplace. In turn, the State is partly controlled by the dominant class; it listens to what the captains of industry demand, and often protects the interests of the dominant class by subsidies, tax privileges and so on, even while it imposes heavy taxes on working people. The Canadian tax structure is such that Federal budgets for many decades, and increasingly so under the Progressive Conservative government, have repeatedly taken far more money from poor and middle-income people than from the rich or from corporations.

It is only within such a theoretical framework that we can adequately grasp the real ideological battles that are waged everyday in this country between workers and the State, and workers and the capitalist class. In this framework, it comes as no surprise that 'days lost in strikes in Canada per 1000 workers has recently been higher than in any country in the West with the exception of Italy, amounting to an average of some five million working days lost and 400,000 strikers per year in the 1970's.'[17] Through a legitimizing ideology, designed to shroud the role of the State, the dominant class promotes and justifies the existence of the State, and justifies its exploitative behavior toward the subordinate class. This class, more often than not, accepts the ideology as valid and legitimate. It is the basis of mass loyalty in the capitalist democracies. The capitalist State does not engage in activities or policies which impede, or reveal, the structural aspects of the private capital accumulation process. On the contrary, the State functions in such a way as to facilitate the structural prerequisites of the private accumulation process. It is clearly a myth, then, that the State under capitalism is neutral.

Any interpretive analysis of modern Statism will show that it regulates the economy as a whole in the interest of the ruling class and the corporations. The clearest illustration of this is in the way the capitalist States are quick to apply economic sanctions

The Critical Project

to socialist countries whenever those countries are deemed to have transgressed. But where the transgressions occur in the so-called 'free world,' that is, capitalist world, such as South Africa, we are assured that sanctions never achieve anything.

In June 1986, at the height of the South Africa's regime's suppression of all kinds of freedoms, including suppression of news reporting, an international United Nations five-day conference attended by 132 States called for mandatory economic sanctions against South Africa, as the only alternative to further violence in that country. The United States, Britain, and West Germany didn't even take part in the conference. It has to be understood, then, that for all their fanfare about 'human rights' and the dignity of humankind, these non-participant nations (South Africa's main trading partners, of course) are more concerned with ensuring the uninterrupted flow of economic surplus from the exploited labor of Black South Africans, than with helping to cultivate an atmosphere for the enhancement of human dignity. In this sort of political context, one is inclined to accept fully Marx's analysis of the capitalist State as nothing more than the form of organization which the bourgeoisie necessarily adopts for the mutual guarantee of their prosperity and interests.

The fiscal crisis of the Canadian State is due to its increasing social welfare role and in trying to balance manifestly contradictory objects. It wants to maintain the capitalist structure intact; it wants to stimulate private economic expansion; it wants to keep inflation down; it wants to maintain an 'acceptable' level of unemployment; and at the same time attend to the economic and social welfare of all citizens. All of the programs of the capitalist State are aimed specifically at justifying the existing arrangement and diffusing the built-in crises. There is little point to the discussion of modern capitalist politics, such as in Canada, which leaves out a serious analysis of the State as it facilitates the private accumulation of capital and economic power.

What has to be understood is that the capitalist State, for all its outward show of autonomy and muscle-flexing, depends on privatization: for organizing production, for the continuous private accumulation of capital and wealth, from which revenues are derived to finance the State's political ends.

Dilemmas and Contradictions in Social Theory

Because the State depends upon the private accumulation process, in turn it does things which please and satisfy the captains of industry rather than the electorate. Periodic 'democratic' elections or change of governments do nothing to change this fact. Indeed, the growing power of the Executive branch and the declining power of the elected 'Legislative' branch in the leading liberal democracies is indicative of this reality. The structure of the capitalist State is such that it must kowtow to the interests of the capitalist class from which it derives a good deal of its revenues. The cruel irony is that in the political groveling involving the State and the 'private sector' the consumer in the capitalist marketplace is twice bitten - caught, as it were, between the jaws of a gigantic pincer. The consumer faces double jeopardy.

It may very well be, as James O'Connor points out, that a capitalist State that openly uses its coercive powers to help one class accumulate capital at the expense of other classes loses its legitimacy and hence seriously undermines the basis of its loyalty and support.[18] If that is so, then recent attitudes of some capitalist States such as in North America and in Britain, especially towards groups such as organized labor, mark a peculiarly ugly and new level of belligerence and menacing arrogance on the part of the State. What seems manifest is that the State shows greater and greater contempt for the electorate, and more and more eagerness to satisfy the ideal wishes of the 'private sector.'

All in all, this analysis offers an analytic understanding of the relationship between the capitalist State and the dominant class, and thereby sheds light on the relationship between individual existence and social reality. There is no shortage of empirical evidence to demonstrate the close relationship and affinity between the Canadian State and the capitalist class.[19] Indeed, we cannot begin to make any sense of the reality of our condition unless we grasp that 'the general affinity means that the State in Canada is predisposed to ensure the general interests of capitalists and assure capitalists that the conditions necessary for the orderly extraction of economic surplus into their hands are provided.'[20] It is obviously a myth that a 'free enterprise' system minimizes the role of the State.

The sociological challenge is that of asking new

The Critical Project

questions; questions of how we can come to know and understand the nature of society and politics. Only these new questions will take us beyond the fog of mystification and distortion, to new knowledge. Only questions of the kind which critical theorists have consistently asked and sought to answer will disclose the many decisive ways in which the corporate elite through their roles as captains of industry, media elites, as members of advisory and regulatory boards, not to mention as financial contributions to the major 'free enterprise' political parties, shape public policies in ways which create the conditions for their self-aggrandizement. Held and Simon provide an elegant and profoundly telling summary to our discussion. It is worth quoting at length:

> One salient feature of organized capitalism is the enlargement of the administrative sub-system due to increased state intervention, both in the market mechanism itself and in the patterns of everyday life generally. In terms of its economic intervention, the state acts both to safeguard and maintain the economic process through (attempted) avoidance of instabilities and to replace the market mechanism where the economic process has produced unintended dysfunctional consequences ... The state utilizes such measures as price control, interest regulation, tax rebates, etc. The replacement functions of the state include bolstering non-competitive sectors through government consumption, acting to improve both the material and immaterial infrastructure of society (transportation, communication, education, etc.), relieving the costs of social damages due to private enterprise (welfare, unemployment, pollution, etc.) and helping to maintain foreign markets.
>
> With the increase of state activity, areas of social interaction which had previously seemed to operate according to natural, lawlike consequences of the market no longer appear to do so. Certain types of social phenomena are increasingly seen to be the consequences of political decision and manipulation ... Thus a restructuring of the

Dilemmas and Contradictions in Social Theory

> legitimation sub-system [which] is required ... has generally occurred through an increasing system of formal democracy in which mass loyalty is created without allowing for genuine participation in administrative decisions. Instruments whereby this has been accomplished include the use of the media and public relations and the creation of the ethos of 'the expert.'[21]

We have only just begun to fathom the burning necessity of understanding the capitalist State. If we are to understand the modern capitalist structures, and our place in them, the analysis of the State can no longer remain on the margins of social theory.

(b) **The culture industry**

For the critical theorists, the rise of the culture industry signals the eclipse of critical reflection. This industry is epitomized in mass advertising, mass entertainment and mass distraction, all of which anaesthetize the injuries of sexism, racism and class domination. This is the nub of the reified, phony, non-spontaneous popular culture so pervasive today. The central thesis here is that with the growth of technology, capitalist society has produced a new phenomenon in the shape of uniform prepackaged and debased 'mass culture,' which under the conditions of advanced capitalism, is simply the reproduction of capitalist ideology and class domination. More than that, Horkheimer and Adorno argue that the so-called enlightened liberal morality is barbaric: technological progress is in many ways retrogressive. Overall, the net effect of modern mass-produced and standardized popular culture is that of pacifying and stupefying people, of absorbing and silencing criticism. Thus, for example, the triumph of advertising in the culture industry is that consumers feel compelled to buy and use products; they make a fetish of purchasing commodities, even though they see through them.[22]

Advertising feeds the terror of consumerism, and at the core of the capitalist marketplace is the norm of possessive individualism. This explains why we never have TV programs, not even the serious cultural and educational ones, unless corporate sponsors are involved. What does it mean that these programs are sponsored? Ostensibly, the corporation is paying for

The Critical Project

the air time. In return, it gets a unique opportunity to legitimize itself, and to impress upon viewers the need to consume its products. Ironically, much of this heavy advertising and marketing costs can either be written off in the tax return, or passed on to the consumers.

The triumph of advertising amounts to the fact that advertising serves not so much to advertise products, but to promote consumption as a way of life. The real aim of advertising, especially as perfected by the multinational corporations, is not to promote one product over another (usually they are made by the same company). Rather, the aim is to convince the consumer of the need for these products. Modern-day advertising pander to the multiple frustrations and anxieties that people experience in everyday life. In this context, the deficit spending induced by hard-sell advertising, whereby people regularly spend more than they are earning, seems innocent enough. But above all, it facilitates the savings of the profit-earning classes. Consumption, thus understood, serves as an alternative to protest and rebellion. The alienated worker, instead of attempting to change the conditions of his/her work-world, seeks renewal and solace in the latest fad or fashion, or the newest gadget available for mass consumption. Why change the world, when you can learn to adjust to a raw deal?

In the capitalist economy, artificially created needs are made into ideals by such well-known strategies as advertising and credit. We are constantly being socialized by the multi-billion dollar advertising industry to strive to fulfill these 'needs.' In 1978, Proctor and Gamble, one of the three multinational corporations which control 90% of the home cleaning and soap market spent $554 million (U.S.) a year on advertising.[23] Indeed, such advertisement has to be considered as a wanton waste of resources. The corporation fervently encourages the consumer to choose this brand of commodity over that, when both are in fact produced by the same company. It is a bogus choice. But in doing so, the corporation also succeeds in moulding the consumer into compulsive consumption.

In the commodity market, commodities are realized by individuals as abstract things, quite apart from the actual relationships by which those objects are produced and subsequently exchanged. The commodity is a part of a larger whole, a totality, which is

Dilemmas and Contradictions in Social Theory

effectively hidden from consciousness. False as well as genuine needs are usually **individualized**, as for example, the way in which the popular concern for health is individualized, or privatized: if one's respiratory system is rendered faulty by a polluted atmosphere, one must nevertheless deal with it as a private misfortune which must be dealt with individually; not a public issue, requiring political action and social change. The self-interest of the powerful is the implied social norm in commercial advertising, which is why the critical attitude is concerned with the **ends** to which science and technology are put, and advocates that technocrats be held responsible for the actions they pursue in the name of rationality. This is clearly related to the next concern of the Critical project.

(c) **The fetishism of commodities**

Unlike any previous period in the history of capitalism, we live in a milieu of commodity fetishism. The notion of commodity fetishism represents a theory of the ideology of advanced capitalist societies, for in such societies the link between the economic sphere and the political sphere is the commodity form. The key point is that commodity fetishism makes it appear that the interests of the powerful class and all others are identical. But the mechanism whereby this seeming identity of interest is forged, is disguised. This has to be seen as one of the neat ways in which the structure of capitalist societies gains mass support and commitment. By turning workers into mindless consumers, capitalism guarantees the conditions for the extension of the market for its products. To the extent that workers maintain their fetish for commodities, they will not be predisposed to question the nature, let alone the consequences of, the system as it is. It is a classic situation of the consumers cooperating in their own alienation. The liberal, corporate myth that the consumer is 'king' remains unquestioned.

Naturally then, (and this is what is of interest to the Frankfurt theorists) the fetish for commodities hinders the growth of workers' consciousness, and helps to perpetuate the life of capitalism. In turn, capitalism increases the alienation of workers by its unremitting tendency to institutionalize the fetishism. It accomplishes this by standardizing tastes, codifying value priorities, and generally giving the appearance of unquestioned rationality. The result, in Marcuse's terms, is a 'one-dimensional society' in which individuals lose the ability to think critically and oppositionally about society. They give up a good deal of their liberty which they surrender for material goods. This is the seductive side of capitalism. People are led to believe that each new commodity will satisfy their deepest emotional needs, if not solve the long term problems of material existence.

This 'mysterious' power of the commodity form was long recognized by Marx, who also felt that the commodity contained the basic contradictions of capitalism. Marcuse concretizes this insight by pointing out how modern 'consumers recognize themselves in their commodities.' In today's commodity market we might say that they find their souls in their cars, VCRs, micro-wave ovens, split-level homes and imported gadgets. This is not a matter of speculation. There is enough empirical evidence to confirm that the working class identifies itself with the consumer society, and finds in consumerism its comfort, if not its satisfaction. It is now also clearly established that in the United States, Great Britain, and other liberal democracies, the working class votes for and continues to strongly support Conservative political parties led by persons with deeply reactionary opinions, and committed to policies thoroughly opposed to the interests of the working class.

The tyranny of consumption turns alienation itself into a commodity. And the modern manufacturer sees, always, the need to stimulate consumer demand as a major priority of the life of capitalism, and the cultivation of a mass, homogenized, market as keys to surplus value. In fact, the fetishism of commodities is congruent with the aims of science - manipulation. To the degree that the capitalist economy lives on and is totally dependent upon the exchange of commodities, it subscribes to a view of human beings as objects to be manipulated, for this ensures absolute control over the demand for products. The desired results are clearly accomplished, as Leiss notes, by the incessant solicitations of the marketplace in a double-barrelled fashion. First, by the fact that continuous rapid progress in scientific research and technological application has enabled producers to flood the market with complex chemical compounds, the long term consequences of which we haven't even began to contemplate. And secondly, by teaching the consumer to

Dilemmas and Contradictions in Social Theory

have naive faith in the power of science to counteract any deletrious side-effects by means of further innovations and new products. In either case, the current mode of operation grows on a colossal auto-experiment by individuals.[24] We become, in the words of one sociologist, serfs to the captains of consciousness.[25]

As a structure of social relations premised on the continuous extraction of surplus profit from human labor, and on mindless consumption, capitalism is not known for humanitarian or moral principles. Thus, given the goals and logic of capitalist production, the social relations of the capitalist are governed by the rule of profit, and this implies ideological training in a commodity conception of the world.[26] Because profit-making is taken as an end in itself, social life becomes parcelled into different, convenient opportunities to gorge the consumer and to increase private profits. Christmas, Easter, Father's Day, Hallowe'en, Valentine's Day, Mother's Day, and so on, all become opportunities for capitalism's triumph. And cliches such as 'what the market will bear' serve only as an excuse to gormandize the consumer. First, something of dubious use-value is produced because there is the feeling that it can be sold or exchanged. Then, through advertising, a market is moulded to suit the product. The process of socializing the populations of modern capitalist societies into consumerism is a highly sophisticated business and one of the ideological triumphs of twentieth century capitalism.

(d) **The critique of ideology**

True to the Marxian project, first begun in 1845 (**The German Ideology**), there is in critical theory a strong element of ideology-critique. In capitalist societies, the dominant class has the wherewithal to lord it over other classes not only by its control over the means of production and economic resources, but also by its control over **ideas**.

Now, the problem is not simply the fact that bourgeois interpretations of the world exist. More pointedly, the liberal ideology of 'fair exchange,' 'privatism,' and individualism, which the powerful class dispenses **conceals** capitalism's constitutive social relations and contradictions, including class exploitation, making it difficult if not impossible for the subordinate class to become aware of its interests. This way, the values and imperatives of capitalism are reinforced, and securing consent and acceptance of the status quo becomes relatively easy. Political acquiescence depends upon the concealment of contradictions and upon a mystification of the material reality. The dominant ideology typically functions to fragment the interpretation of the world, making any comprehension of the whole, or a vision of an alternative reality, impossible. As Marx polemicized against German ideology, so it is today. The reigning ideology assumes that what is, will continue to be the same. This thus denies the possibility of transcending the present, and we are left, instead, with a mere apologia for the existing state of affairs.

This imagery is very easy to concretize in the Canadian context. 'In 1984, there were 546 AM and FM radio stations in Canada, reaching, in a week, from 93 to 96% of individuals twelve or older.' Similarly, there were 96 commercial television stations in Canada in the same time period, the highest number per capita in the world.[27] Yet, with the exception of the Canadian Broadcasting Corporation, the mass media are in large measure owned and controlled by big business, for whom the cliches 'freedom of speech' or 'free press' means little more than a bogus freedom to choose between any number of like-minded, empty and ignorant newspapers or radio stations. In the United States, the powerful mass media are entirely privately owned, and increasingly by fewer and fewer media conglomerates. No wonder they are primarily concerned with selling commodities rather than with interpretive reporting. In the view of American analysts, the American media companies rule over huge economic empires, with the result that a pre-cooked, controlled, largely antilabor and probusiness 'news industry' exists, severely limiting free choice or alternative viewpoints.

In the modern capitalist context, the dominant class uses its privileged access to the major means of communication to propagate values which reinforce its structural position, virtually without competition. Our common stock of 'knowledge' about the world beyond our immediate experience, is gained from and through the hegemonic belief and practices of the powerful corporate class. The most effective aspect of this hegemony is found in the censorship or suppression of heterodox views and alternative readings of history.

Dilemmas and Contradictions in Social Theory

It is at least common knowledge in Canada that the coffers of the major political parties are kept well supplied by the big private corporations. In turn, they call the shots on a number of key social issues and policies.

It should come as no surprise then that when Canadians are polled on the subject of social class, a substantial segment do not think social classes exist in this country. This is because the dominant ideology in Canada provides no analysis of society in terms of social class formations and conflicting groups, and it defines the parameters of 'legitimate' discussion and debate, even while lip service is paid to 'competition.' The emphasis is placed on **individualism**, the idea that somehow the individual can be extracted from society, and this hegemonic practice succeeds when it has produced an unquestioned, taken-for-granted attitude toward how things are. This makes it easy for people to interpret their situations as the consequence of individual adequacy or inadequacy. If the hegemonic ideology were to convey the idea that there are classes (or contending groups) within capitalist society, it would be tantamount to admitting to the historical fact that in the past classes and class struggles have transformed social structures, and will likely do so again, unless history has come to an end. It is much easier to deny the reality of classes.

In this atmosphere, technocratic elites come to dominate public policy direction on the pretence that the system is too complex for the average citizen to understand. And instead of informing us, they typically mystify what needs to be explained, as for instance in what has been called the witchcraft zone of modern experience - international economic exchange. This approach to politics leads to the abandonment of reasoned political debate, and to the minimizing of critique. Public discourse is replaced by executive fiat or 'decisionism' emanating from 'specialists' and 'experts' whose primary concern becomes **means**, not ends, mystification, not enlightenment. As Habermas notes, the 'scientization of politics' reduces the process of democratic decision-making to a regulated acclamation procedure for elites appointed to exercise power on the basis of 'objective necessity.'

As it stands, ideology-critique in critical theory is already a critique of domination, a critique of knowledge, and a critique of politics. Eventually, such a critique reaches into all the areas of institutional life which have always been of interest to sociologists: areas such as the family, religion, socialization, mass media. In Habermas's view, the successful critique of ideology must involve uncovering the sources of systematically distorted communication which permeate and restrict political discourse in modern society. If blocked social understanding is eventually opened, if critical reflection is promoted, it would be analogous to the translation of the unconscious into the conscious as happens in psychoanalysis.

(e) **The critique of science and technology**

The Frankfurt theorists's critique of science and technology is the least satisfactory because the most ambiguous of their critiques. It is ambiguous because they have not always made it clear how we might justifiably criticize these. To the ordinary citizen, science and technology have done wonderful and miraculous things for us, and therefore to criticize them is folly, unless one wants to be considered as some sort of anachronism or romantic idealist.

Theirs, however, is not a narrow anti-scientific stance or silly romanticism. To the degree that science and technology have become major means of domination and mystification in modern capitalism, they are to be subjected to sustained criticism like all the other forms of domination. In this discussion, we will situate modern science and technology in the sort of human context that will disclose how they serve as major forces of domination in the modern world.

As with Marx, the Frankfurt scholars are fully conscious that science and technology have boundless potential for enhancing the human condition, if utilized responsibly and humanely. But to the degree that science, as the organizational side of capitalism, dovetails with technology, as the objectification of social knowledge in the form of machines and routines, they both pursue a rationality of means, at the expense of the rationality of **ends**. When this happens, the social responsibility of science may be routinely sacrificed. We may thus use the vast potential of science and technology to supply dubious, even false 'needs,' through marginal differentiation and bogus choices - 23 brands of similar soap powder, or toothpaste, where one or two could suffice. The artificially-created needs are 'false' because they are not anthropologically necessary.

In his famous essay contesting Weber, Marcuse argues that what Weber calls rationalization does not realize rationality as such, but merely an unacknowledged form of political domination - a form sustained by science and technology, by virtue of their intrinsic link to technical control. This rationality has become so matured and complete that it no longer appears to be domination. Marcuse therefore suggests that emancipation from this form of domination is conditional upon a transformation in the very structure of science and technology. He argued that a new science and new technology could operate not as instruments of domination and oppression, but as instruments of liberation and freedom.

Science and technology can be responsibly used for the humanization of society and the world. And this is their strong appeal; this is what most of us have come to expect of them, and perceive them as doing. But the Frankfurt theorists note that these ends can only come about to the degree that the relations of human beings with nature, and with one another, are constituted by intelligent openness and critical responsibility. Where technical rationality becomes the leading principle, and is regarded as the only form of rationality, we may sacrifice social responsibility. The well-known practices of corporations in evading labor laws, pollution laws, or consumer protection laws, are good illustrations of this point. In fact, so flimsy is the sense of corporate responsibility, that where multinational corporations come to view basic regulatory laws as 'too restrictive' they quickly relocate elsewhere, such as in the Third World, where laws circumscribing the ransaking of the environment, or the eco-system, are either weak or non-existent.

Those who practise strict adherence to technical or instrumental rationality would perceive nothing problematic with such maneuvers. Rather, the position would likely to be taken that if in the pursuit of business activity a few rivers are polluted here, a few lakes are poisoned there, and the air is rendered dangerous to breathe, that is a normal consequence of 'progress.' Entrepreneurs in Atlantic Canada constantly complain that Federal environmental laws work against their (and the government's) effort to

The Critical Project

attract industry to the region. These entrepreneurs want the government to relax its waste regulation for Atlantic Canada, for instance. If that is done, they contend, the region would have a competitive advantage over central Canada. Thus, a 'competitive advantage' has for them a higher priority than a safe, clean environment. This kind of logic is all too common in Chambers of Commerce and Rotary Clubs's speeches. The bedrock is a technological ideology.

The 'discommodities,' as Leiss called the residuals or undesired things which come from our fixation on ransacking the environment for more and better resources, are typically regarded as the results of the normal business activity of professionals.[28] Besides, if we become concerned about the foul air, eye-drops are sold to 'solve' the problem of air pollution. And the State usually agrees with such assessments. This is why corporations can plead guilty to widespread and negligent destruction of the eco-system and still receive little more than a 'slap on the wrist' - a $16,000 fine in a case involving a well-known chemical corporation in Ontario in 1986.[29] In the end, it is the consumer who pays for the cost of managing the discommodities, as the costs incurred by the industry in question are passed on to the consumer in the form of higher prices for commodities. The consumer faces double jeopardy, again.

A life dominated by **technique**, in Jacques Ellul's phrase, is not necessarily happy, for even the outward show of happiness is bought at the expense of total acquiescence. In other words, technological society, by its very nature is inherently amoral. It requires men and women to be content with what they are required to like.[30] For those who are not content, it provides multiple distractions, at a profit, and sustains such distractions by well-honed ideological reasons which somehow point to the need for these in 'human nature.'

Technological society educates men and women to want new and more commodities as the definition of well-being, and then it engages in the production of objects whose usefulness becomes questionable. It teaches men and women that capitalist production is rational and immediately sets about destroying the productive forces by irrevocably destroying the eco-system. Herein lies one of the outstanding contradictions of the capitalist system in the twentieth century. There is, Horkheimer and Adorno

Dilemmas and Contradictions in Social Theory

note, a basic dilemma and high irony in the Dialectic of Enlightenment. Science and technology promise the good life, the free society, the material preconditions of progress, but at the expense of the repression of the erotic and subjective conditions of humanity.[31]

The homogenized consumer provides a good illustration of this point. Shaped to the image of the 'good life' held out by mass advertising, we are hardly aware of the 'repressive tolerance' that surrounds us. Repressive tolerance amounts to a situation in modern society, where, under the banner of science and technology as major means of mystification and domination, we have reached the point of exercising great tolerance toward that which is radically evil. The benevolent tolerance toward outright deception in politics, toward the suppression of alternative social visions, and the acceptance of extreme irrationality in the name of technical, abstract procedures, are but part of this larger malaise deep within modern capitalist societies. In all such societies we confront the bogus ideology of 'free choice,' when in fact we have effectively surrendered much of our liberty to someone, or something.

Modern bourgeois ideology uses the legal facade of free choice and fairness to conceal the reality of coercion, social control and intolerance toward legitimate protest. We have, in short, achieved the highest threshold of tolerance for such practices as discrimination, inequality and relationships of exploitation. The destruction of the culture of the individual by the consumer society is a singular success of technological society. For compensation, we have marginal differentiation - the illusion that we do have **choices**, especially as between one commodity and the next. The freedom to consume is mistaken for freedom itself. The more fundamental question of how bogus the choices are, and who owns the stores in which we buy, or the agribusiness that supplies the stores, or who controls the housing market, or the media which impress upon us the need to consume more of every commodity, is never posed seriously in the general **ennui** of the consumer society. If the 20th century vaunts an ideology of life, liberty, and the pursuit of happiness, then critical theory poses the uncomfortable question of why no other century has witnessed such massive destruction of human life and nature by human beings.[32]

The Critical Project

A major conclusion from the efforts of the Frankfurt School is that all scientific knowledge about social reality carries with it, implicitly or not, certain ideological, political and evaluative convictions. Scientific inquiry cannot be divorced from social and cognitive interests.[33] Furthermore, all knowledge in the social sciences is infused with unavoidable value premises, and as such cannot be taken as disinterestedly 'value-free.' Indeed, even the most apparently neutral methodology - the methodology of the natural sciences - when it is applied to the social world, becomes political in its findings and implications.[34] Social theory cannot dodge this conclusion. Karl Popper, that well-known champion of science and the principles of verification, reminds us that science never starts from scratch; it can never be described as free from assumptions, for at every moment it presupposes a horizon of expectations. Thus, today's science is built upon yesterday's science; and yesterday's science in turn, is based on the science of the day before. And the oldest scientific theories are built on pre-scientific myths, and these, in turn, on still older expectations.[35]

A similar theme runs through the meta-theoretical scheme of Jurgen Habermas. In his discussion of types of science, Habermas reasoned that the different kinds of theory can be distinguished according to their formative processes and their knowledge-constitutive interests. The interests of the empirical/analytic sciences (in which group falls positivist sociology) has always been that of technical control; whereas that of critical theory and the historical-hermeneutic theory has always been emancipation and understanding, respectively. Consequently, in radically challenging the epistemological foundations of the categorical dichotomies associated with positivism (theory/practice; empirical/normative theory; fact/value, etc.) Habermas develops a philosophical anthropology that singles out the distinctive characteristics of human social life. His theory of knowlege-constitutive interests (or cognitive interests) is rooted in this anthropology.[36]

The germ of this complex dialectical synthesis undertaken by Habermas as well as by other critical thinkers is that as an instrument of understanding, science is always at the service of someone, or something, for the sake of which it is employed. It always speaks to/for the interests of some group. For

Dilemmas and Contradictions in Social Theory

Habermas, the empirical-analytic sciences (or theory) take labor as their formative process or essential problematic; their interest, in turn, is in technical control of that process. On the other hand, the historical-hermeneutic theory's major problematic is interaction, and the chief knowledge-constitutive interest of such theory is understanding. Finally, critical theory differs from the preceding two traditions in that its formative process or problematic is domination - socio-culturally constructed forms of restrictive arrangements, including idea-systems.

Critical theory's interest then is in emancipation from the domination of science and technology, from illegitimate authority, and from distorted (partial) communications. In Habermas's view, the degree of systematic distortion in communication systems increases with the general level of repressive domination in a society. These ideas are summarized in the diagram on page 101.

Habermas suggests that it is the singular achievement of the ideology of science and technology to detach society's self-understanding from the frame of reference of communicative action and from the concepts of symbolic interaction, and to replace it with a 'scientific' model. Accordingly, the culturally-defined self-understanding of social life-world (Husserl) is replaced by the self-reification of men and women under categories of purposive - **rational** action and adaptive behavior. Analytically, then, one can distinguish between Production Science, which is geared to profit maximization and for the accumulation of capital; and Social Control science, related to protection against potential external enemies and to the development of techniques for the pacification, manipulation and control of the indigenous population.[37]

Gouldner's recent most impassioned plea for some sort of ideological thinking in sociology echoes some of the points that critical sociologists have been making for some time, especially the contention that what we have come to call 'sociological theory,' which systematically excludes Marxian concepts and categories, was always cast in ideological terms. To a large extent, sociological theory has always practised something akin to the 'selective perception' of which psychologists speak, that is, the tendency to accentuate certain (partial) truths while at the same

SUMMARY CHART: TYPES OF COGNITIVE INTERESTS/TYPES OF KNOWLEDGE
(Adapted from Habermas)

TYPES OF INTERESTS	MEDIUM THROUGH WHICH INTEREST DEVELOPS	TYPE OF SCIENCE OR KNOWLEDGE	AIM OF SCIENCE OR KNOWLEDGE
1. TECHNICAL	WORK (LABOR)	ANALYTICAL-EMPIRICAL	CONTROL AND MANIPULATION
2. PRACTICAL	LANGUAGE	HISTORICAL-HERMENEUTIC	UNDERSTANDING (INTERPRETATION)
3. EMANCIPATORY	COMMUNICATIVE INTERACTION*	**CRITICAL-DIALECTIC**	EMANCIPATION (from domination and distorted communication)

*Power and domination are historical distortions thereof.

Dilemmas and Contradictions in Social Theory

time denying the possibility of alternative interpretations. Daniel Bell's well-known eulogy on the end of ideology is a good illustration of this tradition.

The pedagogy of the dominated is still a perplexing problem for educators in contemporary capitalist society, for reasons which the critical project has explored. We can **expose** people to ideas, and structures of critique, and grounded interpretations, but it will rather be up to them whether they take the ideas seriously or choose to ignore them. We can encourage and stimulate people to think sociologically, but we can hardly tell them what to think. Even when people have been enlightened about the reasons for their domination, they might ignore those reasons. Critical theory aims to show particular people that the explanation given is an accurate reconstruction of their situation. It encourages self-knowledge, and establishes possibilities for change, but it cannot prejudge the outcome. We have learned, too, that the propensity for political action and change cannot be deduced from the objective conditions of life.

We conclude this chapter with the observation of a final contradiction of the modern world. It is of some considerable significance that, as French puts it, nothing on the planet benefits from the manufacture of military equipment except the arms industry itself, which works closely with the State. This is an enormously profitable trade, and industrial nations sell arms to the Third World nations, so they may subdue their poor. According to recent analysts, on an average day twelve wars were being fought, and practically every one of them was in the Third World.[38]

Liberal economic theory would have us believe that this trading between nations is strictly a scientific matter of supply and demand and comparative advantage, not a moral or ideological one. If we accept that as an accurate account of the situation, then we should not express surprise that, for all the cumulative knowledge and skills in the world today, we can still point to a greater absolute quantity of human suffering than at any other time in human history. From the evidence we have, there is no question that we have the economic resources and wealth with which to reshape modern society into a better, more humane and satisfying one. Capitalism has the potential for creating an overall improved human condition than previously existed. What is singularly missing is the political will to undertake the conscious restructuring of society to achieve that end. Thus the built-in inequality in wealth and power persists, and is subsequently rationalized as inevitable. This, after all, is the structural-functional position on the question of structured social inequality in modern society. Given these facts, social theory must remain fundamentally a protest, an existential protest against the conditions imposed upon humanity by humanity. Critical theory understands this meaning of theory.

To further understand the nature of political rationalization, the next chapter is devoted to a discussion of ideology as discourse, and to its significance for social theory. We return, in a subsequent chapter, to more discussion on the capitalist exploitation of, and involvement in, the Third World.

Dilemmas and Contradictions in Social Theory

NOTES

1. See his "The analytical theory of science and dialectics," in Theodor Adorno, et al., **The Positivist Dispute in German Sociology**, London: Heinemann, 1976, pp. 131-62 and "A positivistically bisected rationalism," ibid., pp. 198-225.

2. Karl Popper, "The logic of the social sciences" in Adorno **et al.**, **The Positivist Dispute**, pp. 87-104.

3. Alvin Gouldner, "Metaphysical pathos and the theory of bureaucracy" **American Political Science Review**, vol. 49, #2, June 1955, pp. 496-507.

4. **Ibid.**, p. 507.

5. Jurgen Habermas, **Theory and Practice**, London: Heinemann, 1974, pp. 196-197.

6. See Istvan Meszaros, "Ideology and social science," **The Socialist Register**, ed. R. Miliband and J. Saville, London: Merlin Press, 1972, p. 76.

7. Alvin Gouldner, **The Future of Intellectuals and the Rise of the New Class**, New York: Seabury Press, 1979.

8. As, for example, Todd Gitlin, **The Whole World is Watching: Mass Media in the Making and Unmaking of the New Left**, Berkeley: University of California Press, 1980. And see, as well, the important U.K. series by the Glasgow University Media Group, **Bad News**, vol. 1; and **More Bad News**, vol. 2, London: Routledge and Kegan Paul and Oxford University Press.

9. John Sewart, "Is a critical theory possible: Alvin Gouldner and the 'dark side of the dialectic'," **Sociological Inquiry**, vol. 54, #3, Summer, 1984, pp. 231-259.

10. **Ibid.**, p. 248.

11. See the Business section of the **Montreal Gazette**, Saturday, March 22, 1986; the Business section of the Toronto **Globe and Mail**, March 25, 1986; and **Maclean's**, March 31, 1986.

12. Jurgen Habermas, **Legitimation Crisis**, Boston: Beacon Press, 1975.

13. **Ibid.**, p. 25.

14. David Held and Larry Simon, "Habermas' Theory of Crisis in late capitalism," **Radical Philosophers' Newsjournal**, vol. 6, 1976, pp. 10-11.

15. Goran Therborn, **The Ideology of Power and the Power of Ideology**, London: Verso, 1980.

16. Ian Taylor, Paul Walton and Jock Young (eds.), **Critical Criminology**, London: Routledge and Kegan Paul, 1975, p. 55.

17. Leo Panitch, "The role and nature of the Canadian state," in Leo Panitch (ed.), **The Canadian State: Political Economy and Political Power**, Toronto: Univerity of Toronto Press, 1977, pp. 22-23.

18. James O'Connor, **The Fiscal Crisis of the State**, New York: St. Martin's Press, 1973, p. 6.

19. See, especially Wallace Clement, "The corporate elite," in Panitch, **op.cit.**, pp. 225-48; and **idem.**, **The Canadian Corporate Elite**, Toronto: McClelland and Stewart, 1975.

20. Clement, in Panitch, **op.cit.**, pp. 244-45.

21. Held and Simon, **op.cit.**, p. 5.

22. Max Horkheimer and Theodor Adorno, **The Dialectic of Enlightenment**, New York: Herder and Herder, 1972, p. 167, **passim**, and Herbert Marcuse, **One Dimensional Man**, Boston: Beacon Press, 1964.

23. Milton Moskowitz, et al. (eds.), **Everybody's Business: Alamanac**, San Francisco: Harper & Row, 1980, p. 359; see, also, Herbert Marcuse, **An Essay on Liberation**, Boston: Beacon Press, 1969; and cf. William Leiss, **The Limits to Satisfaction**.

24. William Leiss, **The Limits to Satisfaction: An Essay on the Problem of Needs and Commodities**, Toronto: University of Toronto Press, 1976, pp. 16-17. Leiss notes, further, that a 1975 report by a Canadian biochemist estimates that Canadians ingest about 2,500 commercially produced chemicals

Dilemmas and Contradictions in Social Theory

each day. No research has been done on the combined effects of these chemicals (p. 137).

25. See Stuart Ewen, **Captains of Consciousness: Advertising and the Roots of the Consumer Culture**, New York: McGraw-Hill Book Co., 1976.

26. Therborn, **op.cit.**, p. 57.

27. Benjamin Singer, **Advertising and Society**, Toronto: Addison-Wesley Publishers, 1986, pp. 6-8. For notes on the American situation, see Michael Parenti, "The moneyed media," **Economic Notes**, 51, Oct. 1983, pp. 7-12.

28. Leiss, **op.cit.**, pp. 33-35.

29. According to the report in **Maclean's** magazine, Dow Chemical Canada Inc. pleaded guilty to polluting the St. Clair River near Sarnia, Ontario. While Ontario firms had reported 275 chemical spills between 1972 and 1984, Dow was only the second to admit negligence. Ontario Environment Minister had warned that he intended to deal severely with polluters, and sought a $100,000 penalty. Instead, in this case, the provincial court judge concluded that the fine should be $16,000, arguing that Dow was prompt in cleaning up the spill. And, besides, the cleanup had cost the company $1 million! See **Maclean's**, March 3, 1986, p. 13.

It bears noting that, the 'president of Dow Chemical in 1972 promised that some day Dow would be able to elude all government controls and laws, in the United States and elsewhere, by relocating itself on an island in the middle of an ocean, beyond the reach of any nation-State.' Richard J. Barnet and Ronald E. Muller, **Global Reach: The Power of Multinational Corporations**, New York: Simon and Schuster, 1974, p. 16; and Hazel Henderson, **The Politics of the Solar Age**, Garden City, N.Y.: Doubleday, 1981, p. 97.

30. Jacques Ellul, **The Technological Society**, New York: Vintage Books, 1964.

31. **Dialectic of Enlightenment**, pp. 3-40. Also see Max Horkheimer, **Eclipse of Reason**, New York: Seabury Press, 1974.

32. Matthew Lamb, "The challenge of critical theory," in Gregory Baum (ed.), **Sociology and Human Destiny: Essays on Sociology, Religion and Society**, New York: Seabury Press, 1980, p. 186.

33. Jurgen Habermas, **Knowledge and Human Interests**, Boston: Beacon Press, 1971; and see Alvin Gouldner, **The Dialectic of Ideology and Technology**, New York: Seabury Press, 1976, chp. 2; and Christopher Lloyd (ed.), **Social Theory and Political Practice**, Oxford: Clarendon Press, 1983, p. 19.

34. James Farganis, "A preface to critical theory," **Theory and Society**, vol. 2, #4, Winter, 1975, p. 483.

35. Karl Popper, **Objective Knowledge: An Evolutionary Approach**, Oxford: The Clarendon Press, 1972, pp. 346-7.

36. Habermas, **Knowledge and Human Interests**, pp. 306-17.

37. See Hilary Rose and Steven Rose (eds.), **The Political Economy of Science**, London: Macmillan, 1976, chp. 2.

38. Marilyn French, **Beyond Power: Of Women, Men and Morals**, New York: Ballantine Books, 1985, p. 427; and Paul Harrison, **Inside the Third World**, Harmondsworth: Penguin, 1985, p. 368.

CHAPTER FIVE

IDEOLOGY AS SOCIAL DISCOURSE

I

'It is not understandable why men passively adjust to a condition of unchanged destructive irrationality or why they enroll in movements whose contradiction to their own interests is in no way difficult to perceive.' (T. Adorno, **Stichworte**, 1969, cited in Russell Jacoby, **Social Amnesia**)[1]

The answer to this query is given in **culture**: culture as power. It is given in **ideology**: ideology as culture. It is given in the **dominant** ideology, as that which exercises hegemonic domination and legitimizes the existing social arrangements as the fixed, universal and immutable.

In this chapter, the concept of ideology, for all its extraordinary ambiguity and negative, circumscribed definitions in daily use, is given some attention. The ideas of some of the leading figures in this field of analysis will be briefly discussed with the intent of situating and understanding ideology in the material conditions of their production and dissemination. These leading scholars: Marx, Mannheim, Gramsci and Althusser all agree, inspite of their intellectual differences, that ideologies originate in specific historical periods, and under specific social conditions, as a medium of discourse, in all societies. In class societies, this discourse takes on special meaning and significance.

There is definitely no relation between the abundance of definitions of ideology in the social science literature, and the sociological understanding of it. More significantly, there is no standard agreement amongst sociologists as to the essential characteristics of ideology. Some say it is logical, others deny its logical quality; some argue that an ideology is rational, others deny this quality; some claim that the distortions which an ideology projects are conscious lies; but some claim that the distortions are only half-conscious.[2]

As Kellner so aptly puts it, 'There is no agreement over what ideology is, and the concept itself has become the elusive booty of competing schools of social thought seeking to capture 'ideology' for their own purposes.' Yet, the point that that state of affairs exists, is no reason to despair. 'It is important to break through this confusion to understand the nature and function of ideology, because the concept commonly refers both to those ideas, images, and theories that mystify social reality and block social change, and to those programs of social reconstruction that mobilize people for social activism.[3]

For the purpose of this discussion, we can utilize a synthetic definition derived from Pat Marchak and Douglas Kellner. For Marchak and for Kellner an ideology is a screen of assumptions, beliefs, explanations, values and unexamined knowledge about realities, held by its very nature by faith. Thus, at the core of all ideologies are certain basic assmuptions about the world, society, human nature, politics, economics, sexuality and daily life.[4]

The identification of these properties of ideology alerts us to the fact that ideologies are politically mobilizing and integrated belief systems; that is, shared cultural meanings, generated to structure our understanding of the world. As such, they exist, like all cultural phenomena, in ensembles of social relations. Their fundamental consequences are to consolidate the existing social conditions with justifications derived from the status quo, and to shield and guard the existing society against its own historical alternatives.[5]

In the earliest conceptions of ideology from Machiavelli and Bacon to de Tracy, Napoleon and Feuerbach, ideology was almost always considered a **psychological** distortion, a problem at the level of cognition. No doubt this is partly how it acquired its negative definition and connotation in its historical evolution. The modern-day sociological appreciation of the concept owes much to Marx, for whom ideology was not a psychological phenomenon, but had to be comprehended, like religion, as a social and cultural product deriving from the material reality as it is

Ideology as Social Discourse

historically made by men and women. With Marx, then, came a dramatic break with earlier conceptions, with the recognition that consciousness was not independent of material conditions. With Marx, what men and women think, how they conceptualize the world, is necessarily related to and even conditioned by, the historical reality of social arrangements.

II

Karl Marx

Marx's principal theoretical concern was to confront and analyze first, the fact that the production of consciousness and of ideas is directly woven with the material activity of men and women; and secondly, how bourgeois social science, as exemplified in classical political economy, lay claim to a comprehensive world outlook, but was actually an **ideology** because it systematically excluded any concept of historical totality. His aim was to develop a metatheory for assessing all social thought as it derives from particular standpoints.[6] His criteria of ideology becomes inseparable from a sociology of knowledge.

The **raison d'être** of the Marxian conception of ideology is to expose the fantasies of the dominant or hegemonic ideology that was paramount in the nineteenth century, and to reveal its hidden premises and contradictory logic - to cultivate, in short, self-understandings and historical explanations. Marx showed, for instance, that class domination was inscribed in the capitalist mode of production, and that the key bourgeois ideology containing ideas such as 'fair exchange,' 'individualism' and 'free market' seriously camouflaged the exploitative and alienating nature of labor under capitalism as it pursues mass profits and private interests. And even something so seemingly real as a commodity, is actually something quite different social-structurally from what it appears. Bourgeois ideology mystifies it and legitimizes the structure of social relations which produces it, as 'natural' amd 'inevitable'. Ideology conceals the contradictions and the system of domination inherent in capitalist structures including commodity production. Through ideology, the true relations between classes, and the social relations

111

Dilemmas and Contradictions in Social Theory

between men and women, appear unproblematic. Specifically, commodification as ideology makes the social relations between people assume the form of relations between things. The reification of persons is commensurate with the personification of things.

The reification of modern social relations and situations is closely bound up with the de-historicization of social arrangements. Reification, as a 'forgetting' or 'social amnesia' encourages the freezing of human relations into timeless laws, and human creations into seemingly independent extra-human entities. Thus, in its classical concept, bourgeois ideology appears essentially as a comprehensive world outlook which, reflecting the class interests of the dominant class, prevents society as a whole, but especially the exploited classes from grasping the total span of the dominant system of legitimization. Reification fragments and destroys subjectivity, so that humans may well imagine that the crust of institutions and the ideas that support them are natural and immutable. But all social arrangements are historically transient and rationally controllable, and it is one of the key tasks of social theory to keep alive the possibility of the **aufhebung** or transcendence of that which currently exists, in such a way as to maximize human happiness. The capitalist mode of production does not consist simply of the production of things, or commodities, but also of social relations and ideas. The ideas that that are dominant conceal the working of the whole, thereby making the legitimation of the entire process more easily accomplished.

In sum, ideology fetishizes the world of appearances by explaining away structural relations, thus denying the connections of the parts to the social whole.

Marx theorized that the dominant ideas are always those of the ruling class. But in effect, his theory of ideology begins with a careful critique of, and a reaction to, Feuerbach's misguided anthropology. Reacting to Feuerbach's idea that all the central dogmas of Christianity are simply sophisticated myths, Marx pointed out that ideas do not, and cannot, arise independently of human existence, an existence which is inseparable from the practical business of social production. Ideologies, properly understood, are always associated with groups and classes whose members must

Ideology as Social Discourse

be understood to represent specific interests, ideals, hopes, dreams and values. The historical truth, as Marx saw it, was that the powerful groups in society which privately control important societal resources routinely shape the beliefs and thought-pattern that explained the existing social arrangements.

When this perception is applied to class society, it will be seen that there is no single universal human standpoint from which to judge the alienations imposed by history. Rather, there are only particular human standpoints, corresponding to forms of society. Put another way, the modes of thought that are mirrored from 'real existence' may be given as somehow universal for the whole society, that is, all classes. But in fact the issue is usually more complicated than that. The ruling class genuinely believes in the rightness of its ideas for the whole society, and has the wherewithal to legitimize that claim in its own interests. The dominant ideology seeks to make all classes 'speak with one voice,' and to accept one interpretation of social reality. It always strives to make verbal signs, imageries, and 'everyday knowledge' have unambiguous meanings which in the long run serves the interests of those supportive of the going state of affairs.

Ideology, idea-systems, and world-views are produced or generated by and in structures of social relations, that is, by society as a productive system. This productive system, in turn, influences the way people think. Therefore, Marx insists, 'Consciousness is, from the beginning a social product, and remains so as long as men and women exist.' The problem in class society is how to enable men and women to understand, and possibly transcend their particular situation, given that a holistic comprehension of their situation is typically absent. Since the subordinate classes do not directly control the tools for the dissemination of ideas, they accept the version of reality which is convenient, but which may very well contradict their experiences and work against that group as a whole. In reality, the subordinate classes are unaware of their own interests because of the dominance of bourgeois interpretations of the world. The problem of history is indeed the problem of consciousness.

Given Marx's historical observation that the history of human society is the history of class struggles, the concept of class contradiction, and its

Dilemmas and Contradictions in Social Theory

concealment by the ideology of the ruling class, is central to his analysis. One of the primary aims of his study of ideology was to critique bourgeois society. But such a critique would only be successful if it could demonstrate how bourgeois ideology worked to conceal the contradictory interests of the powerful and the oppressed classes, by the clever simultaneous use of individualism and universal concepts, thereby mystifying social relations, and fetishizing the world of appearances.

Herein lies **his** distinction between science and ideology: ideology hides social contradictions, whereas true **social** science reveals the contradictions. And since appearances and reality never always coincide, the first task of a dialectical social science is to uncover and analyze the basic, but hidden essential structure, and all forms of knowledge or ideology corresponding to it.

In **The German Ideology,** Marx underscored the fact that German ideologists were particularly guilty of deceit because of their characteristic tendency to filter out of their explanations the facts of class domination, concealing and distorting the empirical relations that actually obtain in capitalist production (cf. the discussion on patriarchy in chapter 2 above). A key purpose of his analysis then was to undertake empirical, historical study that would disclose the historical circumstances which led to the formation of different kinds of ideologies. Such an analysis would call into question the **causal origins** of whatever idea-system claims legitimacy; the **intrinsic properties** of such a system; and the **functional role** it serves.[7] His hypothesis is that all ideas originate within social practices and arise out of the necessity of social relations. They are a product of material conditions in society, and of the class struggle.

But there is more. The ruling or dominant ideology will be seen to misrepresent people's circumstances, while serving certain sectional interests. The dominant ideology is tailored to benefit the interests of the ruling class, but the interests will be presented as those of humanity or society as a whole, claiming to uphold equally the interests of all. This is not a dogma. It is an empirical statement about the genesis and purpose of ideational constructions of all kinds. It is a matter of empirical investigation whether there is any validity to this 'dominant

Ideology as Social Discourse

ideology thesis.'[8] No one observing and describing the modern world as we experience it can doubt the accuracy of this thesis.

But Marx was also aware that there are people who might be said to comprise an 'ideological class': politicians, priests, lawyers, and intellectuals. They, consciously or not, often seem unwilling to reveal real social relations, but instead seek always to conceal them. This, in turn, aided the production of thought-patterns which justified the status quo and contributed to the hegemony or intellectual dominance of the ruling class. Such 'traditional intellectuals,' as Gramsci was to call them, not only are instrumental in elaborating and refining ideologies for class interests, but also in accentuating ideological differences, thus intensifying commitment to certain ideologies.

Not surprisingly, then, critical sociologists argue and show how law in capitalist society conceals the reality of the social structure for the masses, masks the class struggle and systematically conditions individuals for their subjection to the ruling class.[9] From this perspective, law is a weapon of class domination; it is potentially legal oppression. Not only is it always under the control of the ruling class in a broad sense, but in modern societies it is ideological formation given legal sanction by the State. It cannot be naively accepted as the manifestation of commonly held social values (see the discussion above on the relation between the State and ideology).

Sumner argues, rightly I think, that the ideology of law is an ideology necessitated by political relations of domination. As a form of social control, the discourse of law is opaque and impenetrable, because this suits the interests of lawyers, who need special status and esoteric services to make judgments without concern for the **social** meaning of those judgments. Lawyers develop this ideology of control to a fine point, but they cannot conceal the fact that law is little different from other means of political control. Inspite of their insistence that law is distinguished by its so-called proper constitution, what counts as proper is a political question.[10] Law and law-making are, by definition, class-based. But the rituals associated with the legal profession serve the key ideological function of concealing the class

115

Dilemmas and Contradictions in Social Theory

nature of law-making. It is then that the ordinary citizen routinely accepts the idea that 'the law is the law,' and there is nothing we can do about it!

As discussed in previous chapters, there are sophisticated cultural accoutrement in modern capitalist societies coaxing or coercing people to consent to the way things are, and to accept their society and its way of life as natural, good and reasonable. This is how populations happily believe things which are manifestly contradictory, and things which we think they are in a good position to know are false or illogical. Ideology itself is a body of beliefs which is to some degree systematic, but not necessarily logical. Clearly, as Marchak says, as unexamined 'knowledge' held by faith, the false assumptions of an ideology are not immediately amenable to revision. If people, by whatever means, come to view the social arrangements as somehow fixed and unchangeable, there can be no vision (or there will be no need for one) of how things might possibly be. The ideas of the ruling class **appear** universal and rational, but in fact are the historically-specific and particularized ideas used to legitimize a given social order and to help the dominant group to reproduce itself. As Larrain puts it, as ideology has become absorbed into reality, domination is effectively legitimized.[11]

III

Karl Mannheim

Like Marx, Mannheim felt that all thinking was socially determined, that is, that thought was to be located in the material reality of social life. Mannheim distinguished between two different types of ideologies in society: 'particular' ideologies, which are beliefs which express the interests of a particular social group, and which provide only a partial and distorted view of reality; and 'total' ideologies which constitute a world-view or **Weltanschauung**.[12] In real-life political struggles, Mannheim suggests, both types face-off with counter-ideologies or 'utopia.' Utopia is to be understood in Mannheim's analysis as a positive thing. It refers simply to groups or social movements concerned with challenging the legitimacy, interests, and values of the dominant ideology. Utopia

Ideology as Social Discourse

implies criticism and change. It holds out the possibility of changing the status quo and presents alternatives.

Mannheim, unlike Marx, was less willing to situate ideational constructions within the material reality of social classes. Instead, he opted for what he regarded as one of the many bases of collective existence, namely, the thoroughly ambiguous conception of differently situation **generations**. His unsatisfactory treatment of this conceptual turn is discussed elsewhere, and need not detain us.[13] Suffice to say that Mannheim's orientation to the sociology of knowledge (locating ideas and knowledge in social structure) was an integral part of a life-long effort to come to grips with a wide range of issues not considered amenable to the canons of natural sciences.

Antonio Gramsci

For Antonio Gramsci, as for Marx, the dominant ideology, or what he called **hegemonic** ideology, was always a powerful force in society which gives direction to and mobilizes human action.[14] An ideology becomes hegemonic when it is widely accepted as describing 'the way things are,' inducing people to consent to their society and its way of life as natural, good and just. In this way, hegemonic ideology is translated into everyday consciousness and serves as a means of 'indirect rule' that is a powerful force for social cohesion and stability.[15] It scores its biggest victory when it penetrates and establishes authority over the realm of private life, such as the family and private gender relations. The concept of hegemony is to be understood as an articulating principle.

Hegemonic ideology always seeks to reproduce conformity, by setting the limits of legitimate discourse, excluding or stigmatizing oppositional ideas and definitions. As the world-view of the dominant group in society, hegemonic ideology (as opposed to what Mannheim called 'utopia') is often widely accepted as an accurate portrayal of the way things are, and must be. When so accepted, its assumptions take on a stabilizing and legitimizing function, even while it fails to explain the contradictions, anomalies and paradoxes of social life. A hegemonic ideology might thus pay lip service to laudable concepts such as 'rights,' 'freedom' 'equality' 'democracy' 'pluralism,'

Dilemmas and Contradictions in Social Theory

and so on, even though these are not realized by the masses. These are the kinds of paradoxes Pat Marchak reveals as they are experienced in the Canadian context. Marchak's study discusses just how populations in a capitalist society such as Canada happily believe things which are manifestly contradictory, and things which they are in a good position to know are false.

In Canada, the dominant ideology - liberalism - fails miserably when it comes to explaining the many paradoxes and puzzles that characterize the society, for example, persistent regional disparity inspite of massive injection of 'transfer payments' from the Federal government; or poverty in the midst of affluence; or the structural reasons for high unemployment in the richest countries. Yet the ideology thrives, and receives the support it does because in presenting its version of the real world, it explains 'those realities that people could see, feel, experience ... it establishes goals that seem eminently attainable, even if there are noticeable inconsistencies between the avowed belief and historical fact.'[16] Besides, (and this is crucial) liberalism never appears to its adherents as an ideology, but as public knowledge. 'If capitalism could produce jobs, affluence, steady employment, mobility, and a sense of optimism and well-being, then capitalism could be seen as a positive good.'[17] Thus, even with its half-truths, cliches, shibboleths and hidden premises, it manages to 'provide positive judgments on the status quo, shows why it is good, makes people feel protective of it.' In parading as a comprehensive world outlook, but which reflects only a partial area of the actual relations in society, the dominant ideology 'legitimates the status quo by selectively informing people what the status quo is.'

This same feature of ideology was long recognized by the Frankfurt theorists who noted that ideology typically degenerates into cliches and half-truths, stereotypes and slogans which are endlessly repeated (not explained) and drummed into people's heads day in, day out, from every side.[18] As Marchak observes, this way people do not bother to question the existing social arrangements, which they see as fixed and unchangeable. Neither are they able to imagine any historical alternative to the given situation; 'alternatives don't occur to them.'

Ideology as Social Discourse

A central component of North American liberal ideology is the Horatio Alger myth that no obstacle in the liberal democracies is so great that hard work will not overcome. Everyone, the myth claims, can rise in the 'open' society from rags to riches. The possibility for upward social mobility is infinite, and it is rather a matter of personal or individual inadequacy if one does not ascend. The myth dies hard in North America, fueled often by media hype of the isolated cases of those who have risen swiftly through the class structure. Myths, those sacred narratives which purport to explain how the world and social relations came to be in their present form, may in fact be very comforting, but they do not always confront harsh realities.

It should now be clear why the members of the Frankfurt School were keen to include in their critique of modern industrial society a critique of ideology as it reaches consumers via the culture industry. As discussed earlier, the culture industry is the primary purveyor of ideology as distorted communication. The shallowness of mass culture, and the elevation of ideological values and interests to the level of eternal verities, not only distort the complexity of social reality, but effectively suppress alternative versions of that reality. The culture industry, backed by the 'captains of consciousness,' succeeds in introjecting in everyday consciousness mass deception about the nature of the world and society.[19]

In the ideological struggle and jockeying that goes on between the hegemonic ideology and the counter-ideologies in Canada, Marchak shows that it is rather a matter of form, not content, that allows the hegemonic ideology to win out over its competitors. It does a better job than its competitors in perpetuating its myths, and presents ideas which seem 'entirely congruent with the ambitions of workers.'[20] The hegemonis ideology is, in brief, far more willing to manipulate ideas and sentiments, and to have people conceive of the world, not as it might be, but as it is. Ideologies (as opposed to 'utopia' or counter-ideologies) are inherently **conservative**. They are justifications and defenses of the existing order; Utopias are designs for a new social order.

One would hope that competent sociologists no longer think in terms of ideologies coming to an end, unless all of human society is also thought to be

Dilemmas and Contradictions in Social Theory

coming to an end. For societies are sewn together by ideological conflicts and struggles. Hegemonic or dominant ideologies always have to confront counter- or emerging ideologies, from which it might capriciously co-opt certain aspects. We see this all the time in liberal democracies at election periods, when opposing political ideologies are given only carefully-timed and judiciously-assessed exposure and public expression, for fear of 'the other side' stealing an idea or theme. Thus, ideologies are always competing and clashing with each other, sometimes decisively influencing each other. They are shaped and reshaped as they vie for acceptance by groups and classes in society. Ideological struggle is the struggle for social power by different groups of varying strengths.

There can be little doubt about the theoretical significance and the centrality of ideologies to society. We cannot wish away or deny their existence or their human consequences. What we must attempt to do is to study ideologies in the context of culture, that is, as shared meaning systems and forms of discourse. If that is accepted as a valid approach, then ideologies can be seen not as disguised descriptions of the world, but rather real descriptions of the world from a specific viewpoint.[21] The important question then becomes not what their truth-content is, but how they come to settle on a particular definition of the situation. The significance of ideology is structural and epistemological.

Louis Althusser

Louis Althusser, for his part, has what can best be termed a 'conspiratorial' theory of ideology. As he sees it, ideology is a structure essential to the historical life of societies, and is in fact an indispensable instrument in any society if men and woman are to be formed, transformed and equipped to respond to the demands of their conditions of existence. But, argues Althusser, there is always a constant struggle between ideology and other competing symbol systems, notably science, as alternative systems of explanation. In Althusser, ideology is conceived as the antithesis of science, and there is a struggle always to free science from ideology. Indeed, ideology occupies science, haunts it, or lies in wait for it, but when the 'scientific' method is correctly applied as a sort of mediator, ideology is supposed to vanish, leaving science intact.[22]

Althusser's structuralist conception of ideology carries with it a negative meaning. It is very possible that we can never avoid ideologies, regardless of the social system in which we live, because they are directly embroiled in political and economic struggles. But he sets up a dichotomy between ideology and science which is probably false, and is oversimplified. For him, ideology is distorted knowledge, whereas science is true knowledge; ideologies aspire to produce error, whereas science seeks truth; ideologies are filled with subjective statements, whereas science is free of subjectivity because it orients to 'objects.' It is quite apparent that Althusser's position is a positivist one, adhering to the claim that unlike ideology or metaphysics, science follows procedural rules and thereby produces knowledge which is verifiable through the 'objective' observation of facts. Science, presumably, is ideology-free.

There are important empirical and epistemological grounds for objecting to this mechanistic conception of ideology. In the world of social and political struggles, ideology and science do not assume the opposite, irreducible characteristics which Althusser assumes. For Marx, of course, science and ideology stood in a complex relationship, but science is not conceived as the polar opposite of ideology which may overcome ideology by mere intellectual criticism. Science itself cannot overcome ideology. It does not oppose ideology as truth opposes error, and in fact, as some recent sociologists have fully demonstrated, science may not be considered a separate discourse from ideology. Both are products of social relations; both have the same object - the material world - which has been produced historically by social labor. Both have a rational core, and are value-laden; and both are produced with a passion.[23] As Giddens has consistently argued, the concept of ideology cannot be defined in terms of the epistemological status of the ideas or beliefs to which it refers. And Habermas draws no tight dichotomy between science and ideology, because the structure of science and technology in the contemporary world is in fact fused with ideology.

A growing number of social scientists are understandably skeptical of the idea that science is, or can be, ideology-free. They argue that the social sciences, especially to the degree that they mimick natural science protocols, are susceptible to ideological penetration of the worse type - the unacknowledged type. Official social science can become an ideological weapon. In the words of Therborn, 'like all human activities, scientific, aesthetic, philosophical and legal practices are always enmeshed in ideology ... the constitution of a particular discourse called science means neither that its practice is or will remain immune from the subjectivity of its practitioners, nor that it is incapable of affecting the subjectivity of the members of society, of functioning as ideology.'[24]

And while the **method** of science may be more or less objective (or be potentially so), the **content** of science is unavoidably ideological and normative. Margaret Osler puts it this way: 'The choice to apply our scientific knowledge to produce vaccine or nerve gas, fertilizer or napalm, is clearly goal-directed ... The history of science teaches us that the choice of assumptions and of methods as well as the choice of questions to be investigated are choices based on values.'[25] How objective is 'management science' as it is designed and used to change the job design in the workplace? And market and motivational research, used to persuade consumers to buy more products to stabilize the fickle market system? Critical theorists, from Marcuse to Habermas, argue that the logic of technical social science culminates in the manipulation and domination of human beings at all levels, including the biological and genetic.[26] Policy science, if it is to be meaningful, incorporates certain values, for the choice of **ends** itself is a question of values, not of 'facts.' In brief, the pursuit of science, both as methodology or as the product of human social activity inevitably produce some results which raise ethical dilemmas for all of us.

Perhaps the best way to comprehend ideology is to grasp it as a cultural product, functioning, as with myth, religion or science, to make the world meaningful and coherent in the face of the threats and contingencies of social existence. Scientists have succeeded in convincing almost everyone that the whole purpose of science, is to avoid ending in distortion, and this purpose, and the practical possibility of accomplishing it, in the long run are the only things which distinguish science from other intellectual enterprise.[27] Science, ideally, has the ability to yield coherently structural knowledge that transcends

Ideology as Social Discourse

the specific socio-historical circumstances in which it is produced. This is part of its philosophical attraction. But in practice it is inescapably ideological or at least normative, because of the very embeddedness of its pursuits (method as well as content) in the encompassing social structure.[28]

A very good illustration of this point is given by Harrison in his recent discussion of multinational pharmaceutical companies. He pointed out that the usual justification for charging high, even exhorbitant prices for drugs sold in the Third World - up to eighty times the international price - is that they are essential to finance research and development of new drugs. Yet there is no guarantee that profits earned in the Third World will go into research likely to benefit the Third World. The usual situation in actual fact is to the contrary. 'The chief ailments of the world's poor receive scant attention compared to the diseases of the rich. The reason is simple: drug research, like food production, is geared not to human needs but to the effective demand of the market. The poor do not have enough buying power to influence what gets produced.'[29] The matter at hand is not as simple and straightforward then as Althusser supposes, and it obviously is a myth that all science operates on the imperative to pursue knowledge for its own sake, uninfluenced by personal or corporate gain or profit. 'Science itself becomes ideological when a particular method of arriving at scientific knowledge succeeds in establishing a claim to be the **only** valid entry into the entire realm of objective understanding.'[30] And modern science has an ideological function **indirectly** through its service in the ideology of domination over nature, and **directly** in the claim that one form of knowledge, based on certain assumptions, was to be regarded as the sole model of objectivity, neutrality and disinterestedness.[31]

IV

To properly understand ideology, it is important to recognize that it is an integral part of any human society. It articulates the interests of various groups and sets forth political preferences. One of the key characteristics of ideology, as understood in this discussion, is its ability to be descriptive and explanatory, (or more properly pseudo-explanatory) and

123

Dilemmas and Contradictions in Social Theory

to produce an unquestioned, taken for granted, attitude toward how things are. It is believable as long as it promises or purports to tell us how things are, or were, and how they came to be what they are. This is the source of its conservatism. Eventually, as in hegemonic ideology, it becomes prescriptive and persuasive, so persuasive that ordinary people automatically subscribe to its assumptions, and identify with it. This serves the key function of reproducing the status quo. By defining a world-view for its adherents, by setting limits to 'legitimate' discourse and defining the issues and terms of debate,[31] hegemonic ideology contributes to the cohesion of society and serves as a social bond on an ongoing basis. That which it binds together may very well be an unreasonable, unjust and oppressive reality.

In discussing ideology in America, Kellner argues that ideology is not effective or credible unless it achieves resonance with people's experience. And so to remain credible it must continually respond to changes in people's lives and social conditions. In fact, he contends, the argument from the Left that hegemonic ideology is manipulative and is an instrument for reproducing class domination,[32] bears only a partial resemblance to the reality, for oppositional and emancipatory popular culture abounds in America.

While Kellner's theses are full of interesting insights, it is rather difficult to accept as valid, in 1986, the thesis that oppositional traditions of popular culture (that resolutely challenge the status quo) and expressed in novels, satire, comedy, laughter, rock-and-roll music and film, 'remain alive within the contemporary productions of the electronic media and mainstream popular culture.'[33] This is an overly romantic picture. If indeed there existed a viable oppositional and emancipatory popular culture in the capitalist democracies, we would certainly not have, as we do today, the almost wholesale acceptance of, and ritualistic commitment to, corporate capitalism and all its dominant values. Perhaps it is precisely because genuine opposition is never as alive in America as much as we think, why a third political party has ever developed there. The reality of ideological domination in late capitalism is not a laughing matter. Besides, I think Kellner underestimates the flair with which hegemonic ideology co-opts, trivialises, and distorts genuine norm-challenging behavior to coincide with the interests of the dominant class. The recent history of

Ideology as Social Discourse

counter-cultural movements in North America clearly illustrates this. We should not be lulled into a false sense of power and cultural autonomy in advanced capitalism, when the reality most of us face tells us we have a bitter struggle yet to wage, to develop and live by counter-ideologies or 'utopias.'

In seeking to 'recapture the spirit' of ideology as it operates in contemporary capitalist societies, Kellner developed a theory of ideology which shows it as a constitutive feature of the social order which is both exciting and practical. He reasoned that hegemonic ideology contains the most widely shared beliefs and attitudes which are incorporated into social practices and institutions. Such an interpretation is consistent with Marchak's analysis of the dominant ideology as it operates in Canada. According to Kellner, the dominant ideology may be relatively sophisticated, the product of theorists who concoct elaborate theories of the State, free enterprise system, or human nature. By providing 'explanations' about the economy, State, education, and other experiences, hegemonic ideology provides legitimations and rationalizations for certain institutions and ideas, and prescribes conformist acceptance. In reality, it is frequent for this ideology to mask existing domination, inequality or injustice; in fact, hegemonic ideologies may degenerate into blind prejudices or biases which often provide a crude cover for brute domination such as racism, sexism or chauvinistic nationalism.[34]

In sum, at the core of all ideologies are ideas which describe and prescribe conformist acceptance of ideas, images, beliefs and values which people have come to share. Hegemonic ideology is transmitted through a complex of ideological apparatuses consisting of the family, school, church, media, workplace, and social group, which, in turn, by their very nature cement and strengthen ideologies. In this way, our day to day uncritical commitment to the normative institutions effectively reproduces the status quo and sustain structures of social relations, for example, sexism, or elitism, or racism, that are decidely not in the best interest of all human beings. To understand ideology as discourse is to be mindful of the fact that all types of discourse in human communities are to be subjected to critical analysis and discussion, if human beings are to be properly served by their collective wisdom and intelligence.

Dilemmas and Contradictions in Social Theory

In the next chapter, an attempt is made to explicate and concretize the ways in which particular versions of capitalist ideology serve as the rationalizing basis for the full-scale exploitation of the Third World. Again, constant reference is made to the central role of a critical theory of society in grasping and explaining major problems in society.

Ideology as Social Discourse

NOTES

1. Russell Jacoby, **Social Amnesia: A Critique of Contemporary Psychology from Adler to Laing**, Boston: Beacon Press, 1975.

2. The literature on ideology is now quite vast, even if it is not all enlightening. For some of the better expositions see: Nicholas Abercrombie, Stephen Hill and Bryan S. Turner, **The Dominant Ideology Thesis**, London: George Allen and Unwin, 1980; Colin Sumner, **Reading Ideologies**, New York: Academic Press, 1979; Goran Therborn, **The Ideology of Power and the Power of Ideology**, London: New Left Books, 1980; Jorge Larrain, **The Concept of Ideology**, London: Hutchinson; Centre for Contemporary Cultural Studies, **On Ideology**, London: Hutchinson, 1978; Joe McCarney, **The Real World of Ideology**, Sussex, U.K.: Harvester Press, 1980; J.D. Manning, **The Form of Ideology**, London: George Allen and Unwin, 1980; John Plamenatz, **Ideology**, London: Mcmillan; Douglas Kellner, "Ideology, Marxism, and advanced capitalism," **Socialist Review**, 8, 1978, pp. 37-65; David Miller, "Ideology and the problem of false consciousness," **Political Studies**, vol. 20, 1972, pp. 432-47; Richard Lichtman, "Marxist theory of ideology," **Socialist Revolution**, vol. 5, #1, 1975, pp. 45-135; John B. Thompson, **Studies in the Theory of Ideology**, Oxford: Polity Press, 1984; T.W. Adorno and Max Horkheimer, **Dialectic of Enlightenment**, New York: Seabury Press, 1976; Frankfurt Institute for Social Research, **Aspects of Sociology**, Boston: Beacon Press, 1972.

3. Kellner, op.cit., p. 38.

4. Kellner, op.cit., p. 50; M. Patricia Marchak, **Ideological Perspectives in Canada**, Toronto: McGraw-Hill, 1981.

5. See Alvin Gouldner, **The Dialectic of Ideology and Technology**, New York: Seabury Press, 1976, p. 9; Claus Offe, **Industry and Inequality**, London: Edward Arnold; and Claus Mueller, **The Politics of Communication**, New York: Oxford University Press, 1973, pp. 101, 104.

Dilemmas and Contradictions in Social Theory

6. Karl Marx and Friedrich Engels, **The German Ideology**, New York: International Publishers, 1947.

7. David Miller, op.cit., p. 433.

8. Nicholas Abercrombie, op.cit.; and Nicholas Abercrombie and Bryan Turner, "The dominant ideology thesis," **The British Journal of Sociology**, vol. 29, 1978, pp. 149-170.

9. Examine, for example, Richard Quinney's essay, "The ideology of law: notes for a radical alternative to legal oppression," in Charles Reasons and Robert Rich, **The Sociology of Law**, Toronto: Butterworths, 1978; Colin Sumner, **Reading Ideologies**, New York: Academic Press, 1979, esp. p. 4, 7, 246-85; Paul Hinger, **On Law and Ideology**, London: Macmillan, 1979; Nicos Poulantz, **Political Power and Social Classes**, 1973, pp. 131-141; Charles Reasons and William Perdue, **The Ideology of Social Problems**, Sherman Oakes, Calif.: Alfred Publishing Co., Inc., 1981.

10. Sumner, op.cit., pp. 275-77.

11. Jorge Larrain, **The Concept of Ideology**, London: Hutchinson, 1979, p. 205.

12. Karl Mannheim, **Ideology and Utopia**, London: Routledge and Kegan Paul, 1936.

13. See G. Llewellyn Watson, **Social Theory and Critical Understanding**, Washington, D.C.: University Press of America, Inc., 1982, esp. chapter 8.

14. Antonio Gramsci, **Prison Notebooks**, New York: International Publishers, 1971.

15. Douglas Kellner, op.cit., pp. 49, 50.

16. Marchak, op.cit.

17. Ibid., p. 137.

18. Kellner, op.cit., p. 54.

19. "Advertising and much of what is generally termed "mass culture" represent a deformed and internally

Ideology as Social Discourse

contradicted corporate acceptance of that which power structures have historically forbidden ... the mass culture is a symbolic acquiescence, by capitalism, to what Freud termed the "return of the repressed," Stuart Ewen, **Captains of Consciousness: Advertising and the Social Roots of the Consumer Culture**, New York: McGraw-Hill Book Co., 1976, pp. 199-200.

20. Marchak, **op.cit.**

21. Nigel Harris, **Beliefs in Society: The Problem of Ideology**, London: C.A. Watts, 1968, pp. 22, 27, 45-46.

22. Louis Althusser, **For Marx**, New York: Pantheon Books, 1969, pp. 170, 232, 234.

23. See, for example, Stanley Aronowitz, "Science and ideology," in **Current Perspectives in Social Theory**, vol. 1, (ed) Scott McNall and Gary N. Howe, Greenwich, Conn.: JAI Press, 1980, pp. 47, 101; Anthony Giddens, **Central Problems in Social Theory**, London: Macmillan, 1979, p. 192, passim; Goran Therborn, **op.cit.**, p. 2. For more discussion focused directly on the question of the relation between science and ideology, see the following: Robin Blackburn (ed.), **Ideology in Social Science**, London: Fontana, 1972; Hilary Rose and Steven Rose (eds.), **The Political Economy of Science**, London: Macmillan, 1976; Aronowitz, **op.cit.**, "Science and ideology"; Barry Barnes, "Science and ideology" in Barnes, **Scientific Knowledge and Sociological Theory**, London: Routledge and Kegan Paul, 1974; David Horowitz, "Social science or ideology," **Berkeley Journal of Sociology**, vol. 15, 1970, pp. 1-10; Mihailo Markovic, "Science and ideology," in **The Contemporary Marx**, Bristol, Eng.: Spokesman Book; Istvan Meszaros, "Ideology and social science," **The Socialist Register**, (ed) R. Miliband and J. Saville, 1972; Steven Rose, et al., "Science, racism and ideology," **The Socialist Register**, 1973; and Rita Arditti, Pat Brennan and Steve Cavrak, **Science and Liberation**, Montreal: Black Rose Books, 1980; William Leiss, "ideology and science," **Social Studies of Science**, vol. 5, 1975, pp. 193-201.

24. Therborn, **op.cit.**, pp. 2-3.

25. Margaret Osler, "Apocryphal knowledge: misuse of science," in *Science, Pseudo-Science and Society*, ed. Marsha P. Hansen, Margaret J. Osler, and Robert G. Weyant, Waterloo, Ont.: Wilfred Laurier Univ. Press, 1980, pp. 280-81.

26. Herbert Marcuse, **One Dimensional Man**, Boston: Beacon Press, 1964, pp. 13, 20; and cf. Rose and Rose, **op.cit.**, p. 8; Habermas, **op.cit.**, p. 117.

27. Joseph Ben-David, "The state of sociological theory and the sociological community," **Comparative Studies in Society and History**, vol. 15, 1973, pp. 448-472.

28. Michel Foucault, **The Archeology of Knowledge**, cited in Burkhart Holzner and John Marx, **Knowledge Applications: The Knowledge System in Society**, Boston: Allyn and Bacon, Inc., 1979, p. 213.

29. Paul Harrison, **Inside the Third World**, Harmondsworth, Penguin, 1985, p. 300.

30. See William Leiss, **The Domination of Nature**, Boston: Beacon Press, 1974.

31. Leiss, "Ideology and science," p. 196. Also, see Rose and Rose, **op.cit.**

32. Kellner, **op.cit.**, p. 52.

33. **Ibid.**, p. 53; and Kellner, "TV, ideology, and emancipatory popular culture," **Socialist Review**, vol. 9, #3, May-June, 1979, pp. 13-53.

34. Kellner, "TV," pp. 26-44.

35. **Ibid.**, p. 50.

CHAPTER SIX

CRITICAL PERSPECTIVES ON WORLD CAPITALISM

I

An area of intense sociological interest where critical theory can be applied as a significant medium of enlightenment is the area of capitalist antics in the Third World. In the first volume of **Capital**, Marx had programmatically stated that 'one capitalist always kills many'; and hand in hand with this expropriation of many capitalist by few, develop, on an ever-expanding scale, the entanglement of all peoples in the net of the international character of the capitalist regime.

This insight is today fully manifest in the structure of social relations contingent upon the operation of international capitalism in Third World nations. Critical theory is the undisputed leader in forging a dynamic analytical framework which necessarily shifts the conventional discussion of capitalism away from growth and development, toward the global destructiveness and human exploitation characteristic of our epoch. As the discussion in this chapter will disclose, production which takes place according to the logic of capitalist accumulation is inherently exploitative and contradictory. Liberal ideology, the ideology of capitalism, conveys the logic as the only viable form, and the actions the only practical ones.

Some of the most shocking absurdities of modern society which are nevertheless given to the Western audience matter-of-factly and without critical evaluation can be found in the multinational agribusinesses. By way of illustration, let us examine some of the facts. The ideology supporting the present world agricultural division of labor claims that world hunger is a result of the vagaries of nature and the soaring birth rates in the underdeveloped countries. Yet such simplistic accounts are mere ideological smokescreens inhibiting understanding of the **structural** reasons for world hunger.[1]

Dilemmas and Contradictions in Social Theory

Today's world has all the physical resources and technological skills necessary to feed the present population of the planet or a much larger one. The real issue is that multinational agribusinesses have no interest in food production other than to make profits. Their basic interest is not a moral or humanist one. Food production, like drug research, is geared not to human needs, but to the effective demand of the marketplace. Through their power to create planned scarcity and to manipulate the international food market, the agribusinesses assign the poor of the Third World to producing food and raw materials for the rich nations. It is hard for ordinary people in the rich countries to visualize this.

In effect, the labor of the Third World people helps the agribusiness empire to grow cheap and sell dear. And by devoting their land to cash crop rather than to domestic food production, Third World farmers subsidize the wasteful and affluent life-style of the rich nations. What do we mean by 'wasteful'? The developed industrialized countries, containing about a quarter of the world's population, eat half of the world's annual production of food and feed grains. The **animals** in these rich countries eat fully a quarter of all the grain; and it takes about 7.25 kilograms of grain to produce half a kilogram of beef. The people of the United States, with six per cent of the world's population, consume about 35 per cent of the world's total resources.

In 1975, North America and Europe used well over half the world's total energy consumption. The Third World produced, in 1970, one third of the world's output of minerals; they consumed, however, only 6 per cent of it. And so the litany goes on. Maybe population control measures should definitely be introduced in the rich countries. These are the countries that consume so much of the world's food supply in the form of meat,[2] and whose profit-seeking value system will definitely be responsible for either exhausting the world's resources, or else causing (in the search for profits) irreparable damage to the eco-system. We learned from the research consulted here that one American consumes as much of the world's resources as three hundred Indonesians.

How much 'rationality,' or logic, or social justice is there in such realities? And what is it to social theory? If human beings do have something called

Critical Understanding on World Capitalism

social conscience, then a theory which claims to be a theory of society should be expected to seriously challenge the dominant mythology where that mythology literally threatens the entire survival of the species.

Critical theory wants us to counteract the flight from intelligence and responsibility so characteristic of the so-called rationality of modern societies. The purpose of a truly useful social science is to reveal the real relations hidden or mystified in phenomenal forms, and **explained away** in ideology and administrative rhetoric. Critical theory is to be understood as a necessary intellectual antidote to the sterility of the liberal theory of capitalist society. In the case of world hunger which we have been discussing, it is common enough to gather from the communication media that such hunger is, without question, due to the stupidity of backward peasants in the Third World who either won't work, or who stubbornly refuse to accept modern farming methods, or who carelessly have too many children.

In fact, the real situation is never disclosed, and is never that simple. The truth of the matter is that Third World farmers are dominated from without by long-term strategies which keep them under Western thumbs, either through induced attitudes that propose the consumer society and the free-market system as life's only goals, through technology the West alone can supply and maintain, or through trade terms that discriminate against the only goods they produce.[3] Multinational agribusinesses do well in ensuring that Third World farmers get the worse of both worlds. We come closer to understanding an experience such as hunger in the Third World when we break through the ideological smokescreen and begin to fathom some of the real social and political forces shaping the lives of these far-flung toilers - agricultural or industrial. It is important to extend this discussion to bring into focus an aspect of modern capitalism which is too often hidden from view in the 'scientific' sociology of our time - the multinational corporation. Let us introduce some evidence about this modern world system.

II

It is scarcely necessary to resort to speculation about the relationship between the rich nations and the

Dilemmas and Contradictions in Social Theory

poor ones to explain that the balance struck is the result of a carefully orchestrated domination of a set of nation-States over others. In what has come to be called the Third World, there is a net flow of money from these poor countries to the rich ones.

In the analysis of capitalism, the Marxian perspective is unified by the centrality it gives to human labor, and to the different mechanisms whereby surplus labor is extracted from the direct producers. For Marx, human labor was what produced everything of value in society other than what nature provided; it is the source of all wealth. But this same labor is, under certain social formations, infinitely exploitable. Let us pursue this key proposition in some detail, making special reference to the global exploitation of labor in twentieth century capitalism.

Under the social relations of capitalist production, those who utilize a great quantity of human labor will exploit it at the first chance, and will pursue the cheapest variety of it available. **It is the user of labor who cheapens it;** human labor is not intrinsically cheap. Multinational corporations (MNCs) literally trample the globe in search of the cheapest, most easily exploitable human labor from which to extract surplus value, and they do this with seemingly little regard for ethical standards relating to either humans or nature.

These corporations are capitalist in structure and operation.[4] They are found only in the capitalist world, and must be regarded simply as the most sophisticated form of capitalist exploitation, operating on the idea of selfish interests rather than the public good. Their motive is not to take an interest in the national well-being of the countries in which they operate. They locate in the Third World in pursuit of mammon and profits, utilizing all the classical recipes of capitalism, whatever their rhetoric about improving the well-being of, and bringing economic development to, the poor of the world. In fact, they often achieve the opposite. They abandon operations in the metropolitan nations to avoid having to face up to and satisfy the legitimate demands of organized labor, such as decent wages and safe, humane working conditions, and to escape controls that might humanize the labor process.

On the bidding of multinational corporations, Third

Critical Understanding on World Capitalism

World countries devote their land to cash crops, and by simple arithmetic, take it away from possible food crops. In Brazil, the traditional farmer is enticed by the MNCs to grow cash crop for export; in this case soya beans, and to give up on the protein-rich black beans which have traditionally been used for local consumption. Also in Brazil, cattle are reared for beef for the fast-food chains of North America, even while the local people cannot afford to buy meat. In Jamaica, small farmers grow rubber plants and orchids for export, instead of food; in Guatemala the switch is from traditional corns, beans and cabbage to cucumbers, tomatoes, cut flowers, broccoli and cauliflower for export. In Africa, choice land is stipulated to grow sisal, cotton, coffee, tobacco and carnations. And so on. The point is that the maneuvers of MNCs impoverish countries that are already poor. They justify their manipulation of Third World countries by pointing to an increase per capita income and a higher Gross National Product as the be all and end all of human existence.

Unfortunately, in this kind of equation, the **human** reality that lies behind the statistics is ignored. Inspite of the glowing image one often finds painted of MNCs, their location in a poor country is no guarantee of increased material prosperity for that country. The increased income in the South American and Caribbean countries goes to the top 5% of the population, while the lower 40% have experienced striking decrease. When the market for cut flowers or rubber plants or sisal becomes destabilized (for whatever reasons) the farmers cannot eat these products or sell them to anyone else. The evidence available shows that the majority of the people in South America have less food, poorer clothing and worse housing than before the coming of the MNCs. The glossy accounts of MNCs usually found in the media fail to acknowledge that the Third World countries are victims of an irrational international economic order. The paradox surrounding wage-labor here is that what little income the Third World workers earn is soon expropriated in the form of unfavorable trade terms or (manipulated) lower prices - usually brought on by speculators in the rich nations.

On the political level, the human realities of Third World exploitation are even more unsettling. The sort of one-sided economic growth that takes place in the Third World depends on maintaining extremely high rates of exploitation of the domestic working class. This further requires repressive governments, usually military dictatorships, or conservative governments that impose austerity on their own people to facilitate the priorities of the MNCs. Inspite of their nominal independence and brightly colored flags, Third World countries are not autonomous societies that have real control over their own economies, States and cultures. The fundamentals of their social relations and culture are in large part determined by the structure of imperialist-satellite relations in which they are enmeshed. Local elites, fully socialized into the thinking pattern of the rich world, are only too willing to attract the new sources of employment, and to take the advice of western 'experts,' rather than to do what is practical for their country and their people.

This discussion is important to underscore the point that the social world is changing profoundly around us, but in ways that we can fully comprehend only if we utilize social theory intelligently. This change, however, is not occuring on its own. Some groups of men and women engineer these changes, and others have to adjust to the metamorphosis. Marx made the point long ago in his polemic **The 18th Brumaire of Louis Bonaparte:** 'Men make their own history, but they do not make it just as they please; they do not make it under circumstances directly chosen by themselves.' For **analytic** comprehension of the history of human beings under the auspices of capitalism, the Third World is a vast laboratory. But for that comprehension, it is necessary to follow the general rule of social theory which suggests that we can understand a process such as underdevelopment and hunger in Third World societies only if we look for, and refer systematically to, the **whole** in terms of which those societies are shaped. The vast majority of Third World social and economic problems are created by the whims and fantasies of the rich industrial nations and in particular the policies of multinational corporations. In brief, the structural transformation of the rich nations carries vast implications for the poor, peripheral nations.

The corporations which spearhead the intrusion into Third World countries are capitalist, and hence by definition, exploitative. Their values carry patriarchal priorities, and they typically display contempt for nature as well as for people whom they see as subordinate. Indeed, their record, taken globally, reveals their wanton disregard for, and abuse of the environment, of people's bodies, neighborhood's, and of delicate eco-systems. And because they are 'private' enterprises, the managers are not loyal to any nation; they feel no responsibility to the people of the countries in which they own factories, and no responsibility to the world's people to keep nature's resources clean. They are accountable to no one who cares. The long term consequences of exhausting important non-renewable raw materials in the Third World, rather than developing strategies for **recycling** in the developed world, are probably incalculable, and as of today such concerns seem far removed from the minds of policy-makers and capitalist executives alike.

The MNCs are not known for their sense of social responsibility. As French notes, the MNCs have power over every dimension of our lives: they produce what they (not we) want produced, of whatever quality they determine. They fix prices and costs; they decide on the future of each of their employees and sometimes on the future of entire towns and localities. When it suits them, they abandon entire localities without compunction, leaving behind entire towns, and a haze of pollution. They influence even our image of ourselves, both through what they produce and how they advertise it. And while operating fully in praise of the free enterprise system, giant corporations create noise, filth, ugliness; their policies cause inflation, recession, unemployment. All these human experiences lead to crime, alienation, and misery. French concludes, 'large corporations rarely take moral responsibility for the consequences of their operations for communities or workers. Nor are there many ways to hold them legally accountable.'[5]

This is not an overdrawn picture. The overwhelming evidence is there, linking the policies and practices of the MNCs to some serious human problems worldwide, but many of us have no interest in such issues. Problems having to do with hunger, pollution, the irretrievable destruction of small industries and life-styles in the Third World, and with depredatory distortion of market forces, all have a bearing on the policies and priorities of MNCs.[6] Also available is documented evidence of how MNCs use their enormous economic clout and their political savvy to have Third World regimes adopt policies and practices which are in the corporations' best interests. One can say that the metamorphosis of the Third World in the twentieth century is also the pauperization of that world under

Dilemmas and Contradictions in Social Theory

the auspices of capitalist private appropriation of surplus value, and the private accumulation of the fruits of human labor. If we have ever doubted the relevance and accuracy of the Marxian theory of capitalism for this period of the twentieth century, we should look again at exactly how modern capitalism operates in the hinterland of the Third World. The benefits of such operations accrue to the metropolitan countries in general, and specifically to the owners of capital.

III

It is convenient for us in the rich, industrialized world to feel that we are not responsible for keeping the poor in the Third World hungry. In fact we are. It is equally convenient to think that, in any event, we have nothing to do with the way the present world economic system is set up. Yet, we are part of the problem faced by Third World peoples. Each time we participate in the frenzy of consumerism in the North American marketplace, we please the MNCs greatly, but we do not necessarily help any Third World nation where these corporations operate. This can easily be illustrated by the way we seem to condemn the apartheid system of South Africa, yet immediately set about buying and consuming more and ever more of the products from that nation. At the time of writing, Canadian imports of South African products had risen to a massive 145% over the preceding year, all of this in an atmosphere of apparent public condemnation of apartheid. All of us in the privileged sector of the world economic system 'profit from it to the degree that Third World people are subsidizing our breakfasts, lunches, dinners, underwear, shirts, sheets, automobile tyres, through their cheap labor.'[7]

It is in fact instructive, and of some considerable importance, to note the labels on a random selection of commodities in any department store or discount depot in North America. It will be found that a very high percentage of these commodities are imported from the Third World: from Latin American countries, Asia, and the Pacific rim, from places where repressive governments keep wages low and labor docile, and where the local ruling elite enjoy extraordinary privileges and power. In the marketplace, shoes of every description are found from Brazil and Taiwan; clothing

Critical Understanding on World Capitalism

from Korea, Singapore, the Philippines and Taiwan. Shoddy radios, tools and plastic trinkets, and a host of gadgets imitative of middle-class life style, but manifestly inferior, and planned for early obsolescence, hail from Hong Kong, Korea, Taiwan, and places few of us have ever heard of, such as Macau. A Sears sewing machine is made in Brazil, so are General Electric clothes iron; bicyles are from Taiwan, and the list extends to cover hundreds of commodities - in fact almost everything we possess in a normal North American household.

The point is that the luxury and comfort which the North American consumer experiences is at the expense of the toiling masses of the Third World whose reward for their labor, given the criteria of standard economics, and the policies of MNCs, will be less than many of us care to contemplate. By way of illustration, take bananas, for example. As with many other commodities, the world's trade in bananas is dominated by just three huge food MNCs, and these companies control the transport, packaging, shipment, storage and marketing of the fruit. As a result, the profits from bananas go largely into western pockets, while the producer countries get only a pittance. Figures generated by the United Nations showed that the exporting countries get only eleven and a half cents of each dollar the consumer spends on bananas. The exporter and shipper (usually a MNC) pockets thirty-eight cents. The ripener collects nineteen cents; the retailer, who does no more than carry the fruit on his/her shelves for a day or two, keeps thirty-two cents. All told, the MNC controls how many acres are planted, and how the product will be priced.[8]

Or take industrial labor in the periphery. To pay a Taiwanese worker 14 cents an hour for his/her labor in producing consumer electronic products; a Mexican worker 48 cents an hour for producing office-machine parts; or a Costa Rican clothing worker 34 cents an hour, in the 1970s, is exploitation in any language, and no amount of magic in economics can escape that conclusion. And cases are recorded where Federal Drug Administration in the U.S. removed over 500 unsafe consumer goods and dangerous chemicals from the domestic market. Yet many of these same products were dumped on the Third World. The dangerous chemicals return to us in the developed world in the food we consume, for example tropical fruits grown and heavily

Dilemmas and Contradictions in Social Theory

douched with chemicals on multinational plantations.

As for multinational pharmaceutical companies, they have proven their willingness to carry out laboratory experiment on Third World populations, where such practices are prohibited in the rich nations. They sell drug products in Third World countries at prices up to 155 per cent higher than the world market price.[9] Clearly, when the evidence is in, the MNCs can hardly be said to be moral entities. Their declared **raison d'etre** has always to be challenged, in the light of their history in both the Third World and the metropolitan countries since the Second World War. The widespread generalized idea that MNCs are a God-send, and an example of the gradual achievement of international liberalism, has to be challenged as a fanciful myth of this period of the twentieth century. Social theory, as a potential medium of enlightenment, must be prepared to spearhead the challenge.

From a sociological point of view, what is significant is not that, in the West, we have abundant, cheap commodities, and all too frequently, shoddily produced commodities. The important point is to understand the social and political conditions of their production. When politicians and other prominent Canadians exclaim, in dismay, that other countries, mainly from the Third World, are competing effectively against Canada in industries where Canada was once strong (for example, in the garment and footwear industries), they usually forget a part of the picture. They usually fail to mention, or make explicit, that it is not the Third World countries as such which are undermining the traditionally strong manufacturing base at home, **but the multinational** corporations, exploiting cheapened labor in the Third World, and usually at heavy human and ecological cost. MNCs are not concerned with the impact on domestic employment or small-scale enterprises. The politicians often do not grasp, or else lack the conviction to admit, that MNCs have their business needs and purposes well looked after and facilitated by a supportive State.[10]

Putting this in comparative perspective, John Walton has recently shown (for the U.S.) that since the 1970s, a steady reversal of the advantages that accrue to the advanced countries from the global economy has set in. And as if these benefits were not enough (for example the cheapened labor overseas, the tax breaks to the transnational firms) the U.S. government waives most of the duties on the products reimported for sale and even insures nominally U.S. businesses operating abroad against loss of property.[11]

Walton concludes that at the heart of such arrangement is a capitalist contradition. 'Organized labor argues that profit-hungry transnationals have unpatriotically abandoned U.S. workers for Asian sweatshops, although they still want privileged access to the home market. The federal government, it is charged, shows its probusiness colors by enabling the runaway shop with special provisions in the tariff laws. The result is growing unemployment and degradation of the labor force, while transnational profits continue to mount. International firms, on the other hand, argue that global competition forces these moves; that without access to cheap labor offshore, Japanese imports into the United States and other third-country sites would undersell the U.S. transnationals, damaging the entire domestic economy in the long run. Moreover, they allege, business abroad actually creates new jobs at home in the areas of management and sales that counterbalance losses in production. Both sides speak from different positions in what is ultimately a contradictory global political economy; contradictory in that the aims of one group can be attained only at the expense of the other.[12]

IV

Critical theory is the theory of late capitalist society. It advocates the dialectical interplay of description, critique, and the articulation of historical alternatives, as a way to think creatively about contemporary social and political realities. Above all, it seeks to cultivate an understanding of the historical possibilities which are open to us. It is part of the task of any social theory existing in this period of history to ceasely encourage critical reflection upon the ways in which our lives are constantly being shaped and reshaped by a structure of production and exchange that is principally based upon avarice, power, and domination. The universal commodification process associated with global capitalism is also the Americanization of the capitalist world-economy. It is a process for which a vast segment of humanity pays very dearly.

Dilemmas and Contradictions in Social Theory

A major aim of the critical project is to explain history as it is made by people, rich and poor, weak and strong; not to distort it, or to deny that some people experience it this way, others that way. If, in the West, after uncritically imbibing ideological rationalizations of modern society we have blinded ourselves to the historical accuracy of the Marxian premise that the conditions of labor under capitalism eventually degenerates into a form of wage-slavery, then we should turn our gaze to the reality of the Third World. There, moreso than in the 'developed' world, people are victims of the greatest illusion of our epoch: wage-labor. There, we will find that there are such people as 'capitalists' who still expropriate people's property, making them into wage-slaves. A truly laboring class is still to be found: in the fields, in the factories, and in the mines. Those who employ these toilers, usually at subsistence level, often think they are doing the toiling masses a favor, even as these toilers are regarded as highly disposable instruments of production and private accumulation.

If Brazil is the 'economic miracle' of twentieth century capitalism - a country of 138 million with a foreign debt of over $100 billion; where twenty million Brazilians toil at minimum wage of less than $60 a month; where eighty per cent of the land is held by only 5 percent of the population; and where twelve million rural families are landless - who needs miracles? Contemporary Brazil boasts of having the highest paid executives in the world. It is the same country, however, in which the top 10 percent of the population now earns slightly over half of all income. Reports coming out of Brazil in recent years suggest that capitalist progress and development there is terribly uneven and mixed. The infamous petro-chemical complex in Cubatao, near Sao Paulo appears as progress to the multinational owners of capital who locate there to take advantage of cheapened labor-power. Given the abnormally high level of pollution related to this complex, and the enormous human suffering derived therefrom, for the people in and around Cubatao, it is no paradise. Rather, it can best be regarded as O Vale da Morte: The Valley of Death. What is good for private enterprise is not always good for everyone else.

We have said enough in this discussion of multinational corporations to indicate that to understand modern industrial society we must understand the capitalist labor process. Labor-power is the only commodity without which there can be no capitalism. If we cannot accept that the historical evolution of the labor process as it obtains under capitalism has some profoundly moral implications, then our social theory would have forfeited its truly human dimension, lost its vision, and seriously compromised any claim we might make to want to consciously change the social world. Above all, the critical social theory that is to render social life in our time intelligible, must seek to demystify the relations of economic production and political domination. We are nowhere near to doing that for as long as we continue to naively subscribe to the view that technology, rather than socioeconomic change, will be the solution to the causes of human miseries.

We return, then, to the question of ideology. The mechanisms whereby surplus labor is extracted from the workers of the capitalist world, require not only 'political institutions to defend them, but ideologies to justify them.'[13] Critical theory understands this as well. Accordingly, the critical project is a political project. Social phenomena never speak for themselves; they have to be interpreted, and in the final analysis the act of sociological interpretation places the sociologist in a position where he/she must think in ways which transcend the official definitions and accepted versions of social arrangements. Interpretation calls for imaginative sociological thought, not merely technical competence in the methods of scientific research.

If our interest is in developing a proper understanding of the human condition, we must, qua sociologists, be prepared to be intellectually subversive in the sense of wanting to probe underneath the visible edifices and received legitimations of the human world. In the end, such an intellectual subversiveness is deeply political, and intolerant of practices claiming to preserve tolerance but which in fact reproduce an inhumane status quo. Marcuse says it best: 'If a newscaster reports the torture and murder of civil rights workers in the same unemotional tone he uses to describe the stock market or the weather, or with the same great emotion with which he says his commercials, then such objectivity is spurious - more, it offends against humanity and truth by being calm where one should be enraged, by refraining from accusation where accusation is in the facts

Dilemmas and Contradictions in Social Theory

themselves.'[14]

It cannot now be doubted that the major structural problems facing the modern world are primarily sociopolitical ones. As we have indicated, these problems are based on the unequal systems of exchange which have become institutionalized, and on the uneven distribution of power both between nations, and within nations. The central motif of this book is that social theory has the potential to drive home the point that the most outstanding feature of the modern world is that of entrenched inequality between and among people and nations. Such an inequality derives its very strength from the structural features of capitalism: domination, exploitation, and private profit. If that is not recognized, then no amount of theory, no amount of sociology, will necessarily make sense to anyone.[15]

It can be seen that in both the rich world and in the struggling nations, the intellectual leap from believing that hard work will result in a better life, to the belief that the entire system can be shaken up by mass intervention, is what is so difficult to make. As we have seen in the preceding chapter, we might look for an answer to this dilemma in a sociology of belief or ideology.

Critical Understanding on World Capitalism

NOTES

1. People in the Third World are no strangers to hunger and poverty, much of it dating back to, and rooted in, the unequal exchange of some colonial relation or another. There is now abundant evidence that as transnational corporations have further locked vast segments of Third World population into the tyranny of wage-labor, their level of hunger has increased quite dramatically. In the rich nations, we do not always consider that such heavily-consumed commodities as coffee, tea, chocolate, and sugar are grown on multinational plantations in Third World countries under conditions highly unfavorable to these countries. This brief expose on world hunger and the politics of agribusiness is based on Susan George's monumental book, **How the Other Half Dies: The Real Reasons for World Hunger**, Harmondsworth: Penguin Books, 1985. See, also, Paul R. Ehrlich and Anne Ehrlich, **Population, Resources and Environment**, San Francisco: Freeman and Co., 1970.

2. **Ibid.**, pp. 17-18; 23-24, 55; also see Paul Harrison, **Inside the Third World**, Harmondsworth: Penguin, 1985.

3. **Ibid.**, 134, 135.

4. The following discussion on multinational corporations draws upon three important analytical works which raise crucial moral questions about these organizations. They are: Marilyn French, **Beyond Power: Of Women, Men and Morals**, New York: Ballantine Books, 1985; Richard J. Barnet and Ronald E. Muller, **Global Reach: The Power of the Multinational Corporations**, New York: Simon and Schuster, 1974; Robert Gilpin, **U.S. Power and Multinational Corporation**, London: Macmillan; P.B. Evans, "Recent research on multinational corporations," **Annual Review of Sociology**, vol. 7, 1981, pp. 199-223; James R. O'Connor, **The Corporations and the State**, New York: Harper and Row, 1974; and Susan George, **op.cit.**

According to several **Fortune** sources, the 20 largest multinationals up to 1984 (most of them American-based) were as follows:

Dilemmas and Contradictions in Social Theory

Rank	Company	Headquarters	Sales in Billions $	Net Income in Millions $
1	Exxon	New York	88.6	4,978
2	Royal Dutch/ Shell Group	The Hague/ London	80.6	4,175
3	General Motors	Detroit	74.6	3,730
4	Mobil	New York	54.6	1,503
5	British Petroleum	London	49.2	1,563
6	Ford Motor	Dearborn, Mich.	44.5	1,867
7	International Business Machines	Armank, N.Y.	40.2	5,485
8	Texaco	Harrison, N.Y.	40.1	1,233
9	E.I. du Pont de Nemours	Wilmington, Del.	35.4	1,127
10	Standard Oil (Ind.)	Chicago	27.6	1,868
11	Standard Oil of California	San Francisco	27.3	1,590
12	General Electric	Fairfield, Conn.	26.8	2,024
13	Gulf Oil (bought up by Standard Oil in 1986)	Pittsburgh, Pa.	26.6	978
14	Atlantic Richfield	Los Angeles, Calif.	25.1	1,548
15	ENI	Rome	25.0	-929
16	IRI	Rome	24.5	data not available
17	Unilever	London/ Rotterdam	20.3	584
18	Toyota Motor	Toyota City, Japan	19.7	918
19	Shell Oil	Houston	19.7	1,633
20	Occidental Petroleum	Los Angeles, Calif.	19.1	567

Not in the top 20, but still gigantic and powerful are: Union Carbide, Bayer, Dow Chemical, U.S.

Critical Understanding on World Capitalism

Steel, RCA, ITT, Eastman Kodak, Kraft, Proctor and Gamble, Colgate, Palmolive, Heinz, Coca Cola, Rothmans, General Foods, Kellog-Salada, Warner Lambert, Gillette, Bristol Myers, Parke-Davis, Nabisco, Gulf-Western, Litton Systems. All in all, these industrial giants largely shape the nature of the world we live in, and their policies have colossal impact on work and its products in both the industrialized world and the Third World. For more on MNCs size and assets, see "Directory of the 500 largest industrial companies," and "The fortune directory, Part II," **Fortune**, 64, July, 1961, pp. 167-86; and August, 1961, pp. 129-138; "The fifty largest industrial companies in the world," **Fortune**, August 13, 1979, p. 208; "The world's largest industrial corporations," **Fortune**, 110, August, 1984, p. 201.

5. French, **op.cit.**, pp. 408, 413, 416, 429.

6. See, for instance, George Modelski (ed.), **Transnational Corporations and World Order**, San Francisco: W.H. Freeman, 1979; and Harrison, **op.cit.**

7. **How The Other Half Dies**, p. 36; and Harrison, **op.cit.**, p. 335, **passim**. This excerpt from Barnet and Muller sums it up: "Fairchild Camera, Texas Instruments, and Motorola have settled in Hong Kong to take advantage of the $1-a-day seven-day working week conditions there. Timex and Bulova make an increasing share of their watches in Taiwan, where they share a union-free labor pool with RCA, Admiral and Zenith" (pp. 29-30).

8. Paul Harrison, **op.cit.**, pp. 348-349.

9. See, especially, John Braithwaite, **Corporate Crime in the Pharmaceutical Industry**, London: Routledge and Kegan Paul, 1986. Also see Barnet and Muller, **op.cit.**, p. 127 (on comparative wage scales); Mark Dourie, "The dumping of hazardous products on foreign markets," in Mark Green and Robert Massie, Jr., eds., **The Big Business Reader: Essays on Corporate America**, New York: Pilgrim Press, 1980, pp. 430-35; French, **op.cit.**, p. 421; and Harrison, **op.cit.**, pp. 299-300.

10. For more dealing specifically with the Canadian dimension of MNCs, see Patricia Marchak, **In Whose**

Dilemmas and Contradictions in Social Theory

Interests: An Essay on Multinational Corporations in a Canadian Context, Toronto: McClelland and Stewart, 1979; Kari Levitt, **Silent Surrender: The Multinational Corporation in Canada,** Toronto: Macmillan of Canada, 1970; Wallace Clement, **Continental Corporate Power,** Toronto: McClelland & Stewart, 1977; and I.A. Litvak and C.J. Maule, **The Canadian Multi-Nationals,** Toronto: Butterworths, 1981.

11. John Walton, **Sociology and Critical Inquiry,** Chicago, Ill.: The Dorsey Press, 1986, pp. 286-87.

12. **Ibid.,** pp. 290-91.

13. Robin Blackburn (ed.), **Ideology in Social Science: Readings in Critical Social Theory,** London: Fontana, 1972, p. 12.

14. Herbert Marcuse, "Repressive tolerance," in Robert P. Wolff, Barrington Moore, Jr., and Herbert Marcuse, **A Critique of Pure Tolerance,** Boston: Beacon Press, 1965, p. 98.

15. It is not to be supposed that the callous exploitation of human labor which is intrinsic to capitalism occurs only in large-scale operations. In a series of very revealing articles, a Montreal investigative reporter having spent several days working in Montreal's sweatshops recently disclosed how this feature works in a number of small manufacturing industries in Quebec. In these cases, the factory workers - mostly immigrant women - toil in conditions that are exhausting, filthy and perilous, for bosses that hire at minimum wages and with their eyes on high profits. In these modern day sweatshops, the immigrant workers are but highly disposable commodities for creating more profitable commodities. The situation is especially cruel for Canada's most vulnerable labor-power: immigrants and refugees who end up with the jobs most Canadians refuse to do. For more, see Lindalee Tracey's Special Report, The Montreal Gazette, April 25, 27, and 28, 1987.

CHAPTER SEVEN

DILEMMAS AND CONTRADICTIONS IN SOCIAL THEORY

I

One of the persistent themes that runs through sociology as a discipline is the acknowledged absence of any general consensus on how to 'do' sociology. The discipline is fragmented by a variety of perspectives and conceptual frameworks, each seeking to provide an 'adequate' explanation of the world around us. In particular, sociology is plagued with serious disagreements about (a) what is and is not an appropriate problem; (b) what is and is not 'adequate' or 'good' evidence; (c) the dfinition, aims and purposes of theory; (d) what are proper techniques for investigating a particular problem. These are basic problems within the profession, and they show, amongst other things, that sociology is not nearly as sure-footed as many sociologists seem to think.

Given the lack of clear specification of something so basic as what constitutes a vital problem, doing sociology is an enterprise fraught with dilemmas and contradictions. It seems that where we may be right, we are not original; and where we are original we are not right. We are told by some, that we have not discovered anything new since the great masters -- Marx, Durkheim, Pareto, Weber, etc. -- propounded their theories up to a century ago; by others that perhaps we have enough theory, and all that we need now are fresh insights into already existing situations so that we can interpret anew our own historical period.[1] In addition, there is a strong ethos in sociology suggesting that, in order to be published, our work must add something totally new to the literature and to our existing body of knowledge. This further means that whatever one is doing (in sociology) must be new and different, better still, truly original.

But the historical evidence shows that the matter is not nearly that simple, as reference to the history of ethnomethodology and critical theory in North America shows. When Harold Garfinkel published his

149

Dilemmas and Contradictions in Social Theory

highly innovative and novel approach to social life (Ethnomethodology), sociologists were, to judge from their public outcry, almost ashamed of it. For some (and one suspects a small minority) ethnomethodology **was** a qualitative advance beyond conventional sociology, at least in some very important ways. It was (is), as one sociologist puts it, the radicalization of interpretive sociology, a hermeneutically informed study of social phenomena.[2] For many others it was: 'old sociology in new clothes'; 'what sociologists have been doing for years'; 'a new name for old practices'; 'the new conservatives'; 'sociology of the absurd'; and so on.[3] Lewis Coser, as President of the American Sociological Association, attacked ethnomethodology as 'trivia' and as an 'orgy of subjectivism and a self-indulgent enterprise' which he claimed was 'a massive cop-out, a determined refusal to undertake research that would indicate the extent to which our lives are affected by the socio-economic context in which they are embedded.[4] In essence, a fresh and decidedly innovative re-interpretation of the taken-for-granted rules that govern our lives and actions was seen as not nearly enough. Wherein did ethnomethodology fail?

The answer is that the bulk of North American sociologists see themselves as engaged in the building of a science, even if they are not always fully aware of the fundamental implications of the **sociology** of science. This means, further, that most sociologists accept and argue for the appropriateness of the natural science model for the development of contemporary sociology, and for the study of social phenomena. From this point of view, sociology seeks to be a science of the same type as biology or physics, where the goal of investigation is to construct laws or law-like generalizations, so that human conduct, like nature, can be explained and predicted. This search for some underlying 'scientific law' in society and the striving for a 'social physics' goes back to the titular founder of sociology, Auguste Comte, and has always taken centre-stage in the development of sociology since then with a number of attendant contradictions and dilemmas, including the dilemma of the importance of formal science in sociology.

According to Karl Popper, science is separated from other forms of traditions insofar as its findings and theories are, in principle, capable of being exposed to empirical testing and therefore to potential falsification. In the Popperian view, scientific method is distinctive in that the scientist aims to provide theoretical conjectures that are falsifiable, and the scientist is then enjoined to actually try to falsify his or her own theoretical conjectures -- hence the title of his well-known book: **Conjectures and Refutions.** When the scientist succeeds in falsifying the conjectures, this should be viewed, according to Popper, as a success, and he/she should then go on to propose a hypothesis of greater empirical content which should in turn be subjected to falsification, and so on. Such seems to be the practice of science; the content of science is quite another matter.

Now, while this view of science seems at first foolproof and beyond reproach, it is important to recognize that the structure which Popper proposes is based on what **he** (and other members of his discipline perhaps) holds to be proper. Sociologically, this is crucial, for it straightaway highlights the inescapable **normative** quality of science. All sciences are intrinsically normative.

Several key points stem from this fact: first, science is that intellectual enterprise or instrument of understanding concerned with elaborating and systematizing all forms of knowledge, including processes and relationships in the social world. But it is nevertheless **one** amongst others, and must be comprehended epistemologically as one category of possible knowledge. Popper, for all his ambivalence towards the problem of arriving at knowledge, comes down squarely with the positivist tradition of science. But he is sufficiently sensitive to the dilemmas of knowledge-production, to the point where he is given to confront the fact that no scientist could be totally free from cultural values. Realizing that, he argued that the most the scientist can do is to strive to uphold the scientific values of truth, relevance, simplicity, and so on.[5]

Second, then, science as a distinctly human enterprise cannot completely escape the normative ingredient, - the norms, prejudices and presuppositions of the culture in which it is produced. This, perhaps, explains why there have been many criteria used to distinguish science from other intellectual concerns, making it difficult to find a simple normative criterion that applies to all times and places. Clearly, there are and always have been, alternative

Dilemmas and Contradictions in Social Theory

versions of what science is or ought to be; that is, there are alternative norms that are attempting to define what is scientific and what is not scientific. We cannot say, loosely, that science is simply knowledge-seeking, for that does not differentiate it from other kinds of intellectual pursuits, such as literature or history. No one expects the novelist or the historian or the artist to call what they do 'science.' No one expects them to follow the formal canons of science as they pursue their respective crafts. Yet there can be no doubt that such professionals have been major contributors to our fund of knowledge and insights about society and social reality. In the absence of their commitment to the sophisticated methods of science, we would have to conclude that their knowledge is inferior, or that what they produce has nothing to do with knowledge. We are, in the end, placed on the horns of a dilemma.

Third, science is a cultural tradition, preserved and transmitted from one generation to the next, partly because it is valued in its own right, and partly because of its wide technological applications. It is a value, and like all values is systematically contested. Finally, we owe to Thomas Kuhn the significant analysis concerning the **social** quality of science. In Kuhn's works, we are reminded that there can be no universal criteria of truth (that which science claims to seek) nor indeed any transhistorical truth, since truth is a constructed consensus of a scientific community, liable to change from one time period to the next, from one paradigm shift to the next.

Therefore, what ends up as truth, or what counts **socially** as science, is deeply dependent upon the consensus of the membership of the scientific community on its conception of what should pass for science, how science should be done, and eventually what criteria to accept. And all of this may be done, according to Kuhn, quite apart from any universalized, incontrovertible data as normally understood. In other words, scientific theories are often determined by other factors besides empirical data.[6] Such a situation is well chronicled by Walter Grove who was a senior editorial board member for many years on four major sociological journals in the U.S. He recorded that he knew of several cases in which authors had knowingly misrepresented the statements or data of others in order to set up a false problem, and a few cases in which authors had actually misrepresented their own data in order to get published (and they did get published). Additionally, recalled Grove, as editor, he also knew of cases in which authors had simultaneously published articles both strongly supporting and strongly contradicting a particular theory without attempting to reconcile the different findings, or even acknowledging that conflicting views and evidence exist.

Because of its ability to yield coherently structured knowledge, science is inescapably grounded in specific socio-historical circumstances. As the sociologists of knowledge constantly point out, knowledge is a social/cultural product, and any attempt to elevate science to a universal epistemology should keep this point in mind. It is not too mundane to restate that science, and the riot of ideas generally, incubate in social structure and in human consciousness. Science done within a particular social order reflects the norms and ideology of that social order, so that if we assume that norms change over time, scientific thought must also change and shift according to, and in line with, new historical periods and unfolding needs. Scientific knowledge, like other forms of knowledge is socially constructed.

The requirement of ethnomethdology to suspend belief in the existence of a pre-constructed social reality, in order to be able to make the process of reality-construction itself an object of investigation, is a crucial one. In this requirement is an embryonic philosophical anthropology, humanism, as well as an epistemological challenge. Sociologists frequently argue that they do not wish or want to get involved in epistemological disputes, but at the same time they claim that their own field -- social science -- rests upon a specific epistemological position, namely, the scientific one. This kind of contradiction obscures the fact that the theory about the nature and scope of knowledge (epistemology) is central in deciding the 'truth' or 'falsity' of theoretical statements.

No sociologist can work without an epistemology, and the positivist position that science is not thought to be competent to make value decisions as to the use of knowledge, is simply dodging the issue of the ontological status of social reality. The positivist notion that the findings of sociology are not thought themselves to be good or bad, but correct or false,

Dilemmas and Contradictions in Social Theory

smacks of contradiction and academic caution, to the point where one might well ask: of what use, then, is knowledge? And why bother with the gathering of correct findings if one is never going to be able to decide whether the end-product is good or bad?

Phenomenological sociologies, such as ethnomethodology, have established sufficiently clearly that sociology stands in a more complex relation to its subject matter than the natural sciences do, and cannot therefore claim to rest on the same methodological or epistemological foundation. The natural world does not depend upon human recognition for its existence -- the social world does. Natural phenomena are inherently meaningless; the social world is pre-eminently **meaningful**. Social events, unlike natural ones do not simply occur; they are produced. Theories in the natural sciences are typically deductive, taking the form of universal statements from which certain connections are drawn -- descriptions are potentially context-free; whereas the descriptions of a social scientist are not empty of meanings and consequently do not allow for the **same** deductive logic as that used in the natural sciences.

All in all then, the world of human beings and the world of nature are incontestably and straightforwardly different. Indeed, human beings are unique in ways that separate them from the world of nature. Human beings possess free will. They are therefore able to consciously choose the goals they wish to pursue, and there is nothing the social scientist can do to specify in advance, or have knowledge of, what those goals will be. The minds of people are not subject to natural laws. This fact of human agency thus makes it impossible and foolhardy for the social sciences to insist on proceeding methodologically in the same way as the natural sciences.[8]

Finally, the observer/researcher in the social sciences is already a member of the social world and cannot remove himself/herself from it. This is because the social world is an existential product of human praxis, created, sustained and changed through the human agent. It is an inter-subjective world. In the words of Giddens, 'testing scientific theories is a hermeneutic task of mediating frames of meanings, and **social science** involves a 'double-hermeneutic,'[9] since the social theorist must at one and the same time mediate scientific and lay frames of meaning. The

Dilemmas and Contradictions

object domain for the cultural sciences is symbolically structured, and accounted for through the interpretation human actors place on it. In short, sociology is inescapably different from the natural sciences because its findings have consequences for human value-judgmental behavior. This also explains why there can be no transhistorical truths.

Ethnomethodology, like critical theory, has been chastized for not being scientific enough, and for its unwillingness to strive for natural science type results. The debate generated by the rise of ethnomethodology and the development of critical theory highlights a much deeper set of controversies in sociology, recently identified and discussed by Westhues. 'For every serious question', he writes, 'there are hundreds of sociologists contradicting one another's answers.'[10] But this is related to a deep fissure within sociology itself. 'One of the major cleavages in the field today divides those still searching for unchangeable social laws from those who have given up the search; those hoping the field will someday arrive, from those who admit that it arrived the day Comte thrust it into Western history.'[11]

For the anti-positivist schools of meta-theory, a humanist perspective is developed as a critique of conventional sociology. From this perspective, 'what sociology means is simply the analysis of **this society**, the study not of eternal rules governing human behavior, but of the actual rules we have to deal with at our particular location in space and time.'[12] Humanist sociologists have recognized, where perhaps positivists have not, that 'sociologists have failed to discover natural laws of social life not through indolence or incompetence, nor yet for lack of time, but because there aren't any. The limitations on our scientificity are grounded in the ontological character of human beings, and in the transformable character of human life. There has been no Copernicus for sociology, because there cannot be one.' Or, as Giddens puts it so well: '... a sort of yearning for the arrival of a social-scientific Newton remains common enough ... But those who still wait for a Newton are not only waiting for a train that won't arrive, they're in the wrong station altogether.'[13]

It is clear that Garfinkel's study, for all its importance in directing our attention to the question of how people manage to accomplish a sense of

Dilemmas and Contradictions in Social Theory

intersubjectivity, did not comply with, or emulate, the natural science model. Its fundamental weakness then, and its unacceptability, according to the critics, was that it had a non-scientific character. Instead of assuming a natural science paradigm and natural science premises about unchangeable social laws of social behavior, ethnomethodology hoists the very nature of the social world, and how humanity is the active producer of it, as itself highly problematic.

II

Let us turn our attention next to the consideration of a theoretical perspective which promises to get to the roots of many processes which characterize our time. It is, nevertheless, a perspective which has been long ignored in conventional sociology. That perspective is Critical Theory. As the following discussion will indicate, critical theory, like ethnomethodology, has been criticized for not being scientific enough, and for that reason, among others, it has been severely neglected as a viable and theoretically rewarding perspective for the understanding of the on-going historical drama of human social development.

To comprehend some of the dilemmas and contradictions in contemporary social theory it is important to recognize that one of the real problems for the 1980s is still the systematic neglect of critical theory, inspite of the fact that such a theory has provided new insights and thrown fresh light upon many features of modern societies, and upon the contradictory forces at work within such societies. We have already examined the broad theoretical project of critical theory (Chapter 4). For now, we want to note that although critical theory came to North America in the 1930s, it was not 'discovered' until the late 1960s, and its ultimately lukewarm reception in this hemisphere is due in no small way to its Marxian political thrust. The neglect was inaugurated by no less a person than Talcott Parsons. For in his celebrated address to the plenary session of the American Sociological Association in 1965, he dismissed Marx as a social thinker 'whose work fell entirely within the 19th century' and he claimed that 'Marxian theory was obsolete.' In the euphoria of the 1950s and early 1960s, critical theory was effectively submerged

Dilemmas and Contradictions

in North America, but with the impact of the New Left, it surfaced in the late 1960s and early 1970s, even though at a very abstract and 'dry' level - mostly at the ethereal level of the history of ideas, somewhat divorced from ordinary people's actual experiences and mundane problems.

Other important and challenging scholarship on the structure of social inequality in industrial societies were conveniently omitted as well from syllabuses and reading lists in university courses everywhere. Oliver C. Cox's monumental **Caste, Class and Race**,[14] is perhaps the best-known example of this neglect. The nature and exercise of power, whether by an economic elite, or by a relatively autonomous state, in contemporary societies, are among the most important and least agreed upon phenomenon in contemporary social science. Cox's work was an immensely enlightening and accurate analysis of this issue. It was nevertheless ignored. But let us return to critical theory.

The pattern of neglect of critical sociology is now well-entrenched, and continues in those who set themselves up as producers of **theory** in the 1980s, as a review of some recent popular theory books will quickly reveal. In 1974 Jonathan Turner published his **Structure of Sociologial Theory**.[15] Inspite of such a title, there is no mention of critical theory or the Frankfurt School (nor indeed the sociology of knowledge). After four years, the book is enlarged and revised. There was still no mention of critical theory, the Frankfurt School, or the sociology of knowledge. By the time of a **third** edition in 1982 Turner had discovered critical theory. But he immediately dismisses it in two pages saying that he 'is not terribly sympathetic to this school of thought because it is a body of thought that rejects the standards of science as appropriate for evaluation of its corpus'! Besides, he concludes, because critical theory invokes a moralistic standard of creating a better world, it becomes a distinctive moral philosophy, not a scientific theory.

Turner's last word on the subject, then, is that critical theory is not a fruitful strategy for those who propose to work within the positivist tradition of sociological theory. In the meantime, Turner had produced another huge volume with Leonard Beeghley with the rather pompous title of **The Emergence of Sociological Theory**[16] (550 pp.) There was no mention

Dilemmas and Contradictions in Social Theory

of critical theory, the Frankfurt School or the sociology of knowledge in this book either, but a great deal on 'objective, value-free science.'

Early in 1986 the **fourth** edition of **Structure of Sociological Theory** became available. The author finally decided to spend one chapter, not on critical theory, but on Habermas. All is given away, however, when he made the extraordinary admission that he would 'try to stress the merits of Habermas's approach **as theory**, divorced from his critical project.'

Nothing better illustrates the kind of intellectual 'hopscotch' that sociologists have become so good at playing. They want a science of society and human beings, without having to face the moral and normative implications that are necessarily entailed in such an endeavor. In the fervent attempt to deify empiricism and to entrench a naturalistic methodology for sociology, a good number of sociologists still go out of their way to deny and denigrate the relevance of the critical project. They typically use the argument that critical theory is too much like moral philosophy; or that 'critical theory's way of looking at the world [still] makes precious little sense.'[17]

With such an ethos still dominant in contemporary sociology, it makes it all the more necessary for critical sociologists to examine even more closely the putative scientific theories in sociology, in order to disclose how these same theories systematically prevent us from understanding our historical situation. They also prevent us from identifying our own historical possibilities.

A few more examples will be instructive for establishing our claim. John Wilson, **Social Theory** (1983)[18] devotes all of three pages to critical theory; Francis Abraham, **Modern Sociological Theory** (1982)[19] devotes two and one-half pages to that subject; but Graham Kinloch, **Sociological Theory** (1977)[20] never heard of it, neither have Margaret Poloma, **Contemporary Sociological Theory** (1979),[21] Mark Abraham, **Sociological Theory** (1981)[22] and William Skidmore, **Theoretical Thinking in Sociology** (1975, 1979).[23]

The picture is rather clear. Notwithstanding its powerful and profound conceptual content, critical theory has hitherto failed to receive anything close to the cultural reception that it would seem to deserve.

158

Dilemmas and Contradictions

It appears, from these latest theory books, on which Canadian students still largely rely, that critical theory is still some sort of sociological leper. Many of the books claim to be surveying the field, but they do so very selectively. Somehow we are supposed to cringe, recoil, and apologize for any sociology or any kind of analysis that critically evaluates the social and political realities around us.

Yet, sociology is nothing, if it is not potentially a critique of society. And society has to be, as Durkheim suspected, a moral community. Established institutions have a moral authority over our lives. If they do not perform as well as we think they should, and are capable of, they deserve a moral critique, no less. If that is so, then we have nothing to be ashamed of if our critique of such a community embroils us in political debates and confrontations. The problem with so much of social theory is that the absence of a critical dimension unnecessarily impoverishes theory as a reflection upon society.

Even formal education which takes place in the modern universities no longer seems to embrace a humanistic curriculum. Social science programs in the universities are more and more interested in serving as training grounds for cultivating what Thorstein Veblen called trained **incapacity** to understand society. They churn out specialized functionaries with specialized technical knowledge, important for reinforcing and legitimizing the capitalist values, not for criticizing them. In the context of the liberal university, education comes more and more to mean simply the mechanical acquisition of technical and instrumental knowledge, not the transfer of enlightenment and critical thought. Increasingly, what is rehearsed with more and more sophistication is the ideological defense of the corporate structure. In fact, it often seems that the academy in the modern period provides very little intellectual space for genuine, spontaneous thought, imagination or creativity.

The so-called 'culture of critical discourse,' of which Gouldner wrote, is really an illusion, for the community of professionals and experts in the modern university seems not to be interested in challenging the authority of class domination, but to complement it. This is one of the reasons why critical theory has found such lukewarm reception in academia. The university lies at the intersection of many of the

Dilemmas and Contradictions in Social Theory

changes taking place in contemporary society. This makes the business of theoretical reflection, and possibly enlightenment, all the more urgent and immediate. Intellectual work in this epoch necessarily becomes inextricably intertwined with the struggles for liberation and human freedom. Indeed, the university has a social responsibility to keep the critical social lens in sharp focus, and to cultivate a milieu in which not just technique and philosophies of growth are pursued, but questions of meaning, value and purpose.

Ira Shor and others have already carefully pointed out that the educational institutions at the lower levels in advanced capitalist countries are powerful weapons which, for all their outward show of being the fountain-head of critical thought, are in fact hindrances to radical social change. Essentially, the schools engage in activities which impede critical thinking, for example the glorification of competition, and the perpetuation of the myth that we succeed because of individual effort. The schools also encourage blind conformity to authority. Their prime function is to produce the kind of people supportive of the system's needs. Coupled with the other distractions which the capitalist structure produces, the major social institutions produce people who have no comprehension of what is happening to them,[24] and who are not drawn towards a critical reflection upon society.

Doing and teaching sociology in Canada is a lot more exciting today than it was even a decade ago, because a modest, critical spirit is now in evidence. Social processes and relations once ignored or uncritically discussed (for example, the state, ideology, and patriarchy) are now receiving serious attention from Canadian sociologists. But the effort is still largely undersubscribed, and much of Canadian sociology is still marked by an orthodox consensus, all too keen to dismiss as out of bounds for the sociologist such topics as the debate over values, law as one manifestation of oppression in social life, and the role of Canada in the oppression and exploitation of the Third World. No effort should be spared in cultivating and appraising the critical heritage. This might possibly restore to sociology the promise of providing deeper interpretation and understanding of the political and social situation of our time.

It is, I think, of considerable importance, that we

encourage people to think about and reflect upon society as the product of human action, structured and sustained by specific values and interests. Contemporary social theory must restate, with some force, the importance of keeping alive the ideas that a better understanding of the historical process is a way of deepening and extending ourselves, which in turn might help us to change that process. These essays constitute a small beginning, aimed at cultivating a critical pedagogy, at keeping alive the power of critique, and at encouraging a humanistic stance toward the social world and the social situation of our time.

The anxiety amongst sociologists concerning the breaking of new ground lingers on for the same reason that anxiety obtains with respect to the 'scientific status' of sociology: the majority of sociologists feel that only by continuous path-breaking 'discoveries' can we accumulate knowledge about society. And only if such knowledge is derived via the model utilized in natural sciences, are we likely to gain the respectability and status as professionals. But the concepts, findings and application of social theory remain, always, contested and self-consciously unfinished. And this is precisely why the **meta** aspect of sociology is so important. There is a strong and persistent tendency on the part of far too many sociologists to view **meta** as indicative of a prescientific state of a discipline, and as such ought to be quickly left behind. But the position taken here is that **meta** designates the theoretically postulated aspects of a science or discipline. So designated, meta-sociological issues deal with the ontological and epistemological postulates necessary to render the theory and method of the discipline intelligible. In our haste to become 'scientific,' it would be tragic if we somehow managed to by-pass the meta-aspects of sociology just so that, by attempting to do a social **science**, we became alienated from the **social**.

III

It is the nature of sociological problems that they are never completely solved and laid to rest so that the sociologist can embark upon untrodden or unexplored areas. Rather, given sociological problems typically subside in relative importance, only to return to the sociological consciousness as the shifting boundaries

Dilemmas and Contradictions in Social Theory

of reality are sharpened or blurred from time to time. The dilemma which many sociologists find they must confront, is that of conceiving of human beings as social-relational beings **in process**, which means that the reality which human beings construct (like modern cities) is fundamentally unfinished, and undergoes a metamorphosis as a function of the historically evolved material conditions in which they find themselves. This does not mean that it is impossible to understand humankind. But it does mean that such understanding must be flavored with an historical understanding of human experience and with a reflectiveness which inquires back into the source of all the formations of knowledge. To a large degree, positivism closes off these dimensions; ethnomethodology wants them open.

All social theory is necessarily rooted in socio-historical situations. This means that objective social reality cannot be assumed to exist independently of the knowing, teleological human subject. Explanation in sociology requires that sociology grounds itself at the level of intentionality, and inquires into and builds on the social meanings out of which humans construct their actions. This, it seems perfectly clear, is the promise of ethnomethodology, and critical theory has built a comprehensive framework, drawing upon such insights. It may very well be that the attempt to apply natural-scientific modes of investigation to the social world has taken us further and further away from the understanding of the problem of **meaning** and intentionality.

Social theory cannot possibly be of much use unless it addresses a sociology of everyday life. And it cannot succeed, as social theory, without developing and sharpening a critique of everyday life. The essays in this volume have sought to illustrate that social theory has a substantial contribution to make to the understanding of the modern world and our future in it. One can well understand the need to repoliticize social theory, to render it critical, and to focus it on analyses of the modern State, the media, domination, culture, and everyday life. One can also recognize that constant retooling will be necessary if theory is to remain relevant to the changes in contemporary society. But the thinly-veiled call from some quarters of critical theory in North America that we should stop talking about critical theory and begin doing it,[25] is a somewhat puzzling and contradictory call, considering that critical theory has barely arrived in North

Dilemmas and Contradictions

America, as we have shown, and where no more than 5% of sociologists on this continent would consider themselves radical or critical. It is not understandable why critical theorists should wish to quickly move to limit discussion on a theoretical perspective pregnant with radical politics, but which has not been understood very well in sociology. It has never been granted a reception and prominent exposure in sociological discourse commensurate with other, less revealing perspective.

Contrary to the wish to stop talking about critical theory, it is urgent that those who would wish to comprehend the nature of modern society and politics become familiar with the battery of concepts and categories at the core of critical theory. If, as sociologists, we are expected to change the world through doing critical sociology, we might do well to first comprehend that world.

Dilemmas and Contradictions in Social Theory

NOTES

1. See Scott McNall, "On contemporary social theory," **The American Sociologist**, vol. 13, 1978, p. 4.

2. Josef Bleicher, **The Hermeneutic Imagination: Outline of a Positive Critique of Scientism and Sociology**, London: Routledge and Kegan Paul, 1982, p. 125.

3. See, for example, Scott McNall and James C.M. Johnson, "The new conservatives: ethnomethodologists, phenomenologists and symbolic interactionists," **The Insurgent Sociologist**, Vol. 5, #4 (Summer) 1975; Bob Gidlow, "Ethnomethodology - a new name for old practices," **British Journal of Sociology**, Vol. 23, #4, 1972; William W. Mayrl, "Ethnomethodology: sociology without society," **Catalyst**, Vol. 7, 1973; Stanford Lyman & Marvin B. Scott, **A Sociology of the Absurd**, N.Y.: Appelon-Century-Crafts, 1970. These are only **some** of the more hostile and intolerant responses made by sociologists in the 1970s.

4. Lewis Coser, "Presidential address: two methods in search of a substance," **American Sociological Review**, Vol. 40, #6 (December) 1975, esp. pp. 696, 698. This address by the then President of the American Sociological Association sparked off a long and bitter debate in the sociology journals. See, in this connection, the several articles that took issue with Coser's narrow interpretation, and Coser's reply in **The American Sociologist**, Vol. 11 (Feb.) 1976, pp. 4-38; Anthony Giddens, "Hermeneutics, ethnomethodology, and problems of interpretative analysis," in Lewis Coser and Otto Larsen (eds.), **The Uses of Controversy in Sociology**, New York: The Free Press, 1976; and cf. Z. Bauman, "On the philosophical status of ethnomethodology," **Sociological Review**, Vol. 21, #1, 1973.

5. See, also, Karl Popper, **The Logic of Scientific Discovery**, New York: Harper and Row, 1965; **Conjectures and Refutations**, London: Routledge and Kegan Paul, 1963; and **Objective Knowledge: An Evolutionary Approach**, London: Oxford University Press, 1972.

6. Cf. Thomas H. Kuhn, **The Structure of Scientific Revolutions**, 2nd ed., Chicago: University of Chicago Press, 1970; and George Ritzer, "Sociology: a multiple paradigm science," **The American Sociologist**, Vol. 10, August 1975, pp. 156-167. Also see the pertinent and brilliant essays in Imre Lakatos and Alan Musgrave (eds.), **Criticism and the Growth of Knowledge**, Cambridge: Cambridge University Press, 1970.

    The uncomfortable conclusion is stated by one writer as follows: "... what Kuhn suggests is that the notion of appealing to the facts is vitiated by the organization of human perception and intelligence: we cannot see things as facts, but only facts-as-interpreted; we see, not what is **there** in any simple sense, but what is seen-as-there ... It looks as if the dividing line has been taken away between facts and theory, and between social science and ideology ... [Social Sciences] must be understood - if it can be understood at all - either as an ideology in some class-based, Marxist sense, or else as some wider kind of ideology whose satisfactions are cultural or aesthetic. And this conclusion is plainly rather a shocking one to have to reach." Alan Ryan, **The Philosophy of the Social Sciences**, London: Macmillan, 1970, p. 236.

    Similarly, argues Popper, "It is a mistake to assume that the objectivity of a science depends upon the objectivity of the scientist. And it is a mistake to believe that the attitude of the natural scientist is more objective than that of the social scientist. The natural scientist is just as partisan as other people, and unless he belongs to a few who are constantly producing new ideas, he is, unfortunately, often very biased, favouring his pet ideas in a one-sided and partisan manner..." Karl R. Popper, "The logic of the social sciences," in Theodor Adorno, et al., **The Positivist Dispute in German Sociology**, London: Heinemann, 1976, p. 95.

7. Walter Grove, "The review process and is consequences in the major sociological journals," **Contemporary Review**, vol. 8, #6, (Nov.) 1979, p. 802.

8. For extended discussion on this problem see Anthony Giddens, **New Rules of Sociological Method**, London: Hutchinson, 1976, chp. 4; David R.

Dilemmas and Contradictions in Social Theory

Dickens, "The critical project of Jurgen Habermas," in **Critical Theory and Other Critical Perspectives,** ed. Daniel R. Sabia, Jr. and Jerald T. Wallulis, Albany: State University of New York Press, 1983; Michael Phillipson, "Theory, methodology and conceptualization," in Paul Filmer, et al., **New Directions in Sociological Theory,** Cambridge, Mass.: MIT Press, 1972; and David Lee and Howard Newby, **The Problem of Sociology,** London: Hutchinson, 1983, p. 171.

9. Anthony Giddens, **New Rules of Sociological Method,** London: Hutchinson, 1976, chp. 4.

10. Kenneth Westhues, **First Sociology,** New York: McGraw-Hill Book Co., 1982, p. 9.

11. **Ibid.**, p. 13.

12. **Ibid.**

13. **Ibid.**, p. 12; and Giddens, **op.cit.**, p. 13.

14. Monthly Review Press, 1948.

15. Homewood, Ill.: Dorsey Press.

16. Jonathan Turner and Leonard Beeghley, **The Emergence of Sociological Theory,** Homewood, Ill.: Dorsey Press, 1981.

17. This is the conclusion reached by Axel van den Berg in his abysmally shallow essay "Critical theory: is there still hope," **American Journal of Sociology,** vol. 86 (Nov.) 1980, pp. 449-78; and in his reply to his critics, **American Journal of Sociology,** vol. 88, 1983, p. 1269.

18. John Wilson, **Social Theory,** Englewood Cliffs, N.J.: Prentice-Hall, Inc., 1983.

19. Francis Abraham, **Modern Sociological Theory,** Delhi, India: Oxford University Press, 1982.

20. Graham Kinloch, **Ideology and Contemporary Sociological Theory,** Englewood Cliffs, N.J.: Prentice=Hall Inc., 1981.

21. Margaret Poloma, **Contemporary Sociological Theory,** New York: Collier Macmillan Publishers, 1979.

22. Mark Abrahamson, **Sociological Theory: An Introduction to Concepts, Issues, and Research,** Englewood Cliffs, N.J.: Prentice-Hall Inc., 1981.

23. William Skidmore, **Theoretical Thinking in Sociology,** New York: Cambridge University Press (1975, 1979).

24. See Ira Shor, **Critical Teaching and Everyday Life,** Montreal: Black Rose Books, 1980; Samuel Bowles and Herbert Gintis, **Schooling in Capitalist America,** New York: Basic Books, 1976; and Rachel Sharp, **Knowledge, Ideology and the Politics of Schooling: Towards a Marxist Analysis of Education,** London: Routledge and Kegan Paul, 1980.

25. For instance, see Douglas Kellner and Rick Roderick, "Recent literature on critical theory," **New German Critique,** 23, (Spring-Summer) 1981, pp. 141-170.

CHAPTER EIGHT

UNDERSTANDING OF BLACK SOCIETY IN NORTH AMERICA:
DILEMMAS AND CONTRADICTIONS

I

Following upon the earlier chapter on ideology the discussion in this brief chapter is meant to be illustrative - to show that beliefs do not exist in the abstract, but are held by people who use them to organize action. In the case of Black society in the Americas, the interests of the dominant groups were bound up with the preservation of the status quo. The racist ideology which was so meticulously developed to legitimize the relations of domination in plantation society throughout the Americas, continues to define the status of Blacks in North American society. But instead of explaining Blacks through history, conventional social science seems to explain history through Blacks. In the following discussion, some of these problems are explored.

Two fundamental issues concerning the problem of 'race relations' in North America will be discussed in order to underscore the point that a fresh theoretical approach other than the well-worn class model is necessary for the structural understanding of Black society in Canada and the U.S.A. The first of these issues has to do with the thesis of the 'declining significance of race' in American race-relations; the second, with the purported gains in Black life-chances and status in American society, and in the New World generally. The two are not unrelated.

Not very long ago, we had prominent American sociologists declaring that the concept of social class was no longer relevant to the analysis of American society. Robert Nisbet, for instance, argued that 'however useful social classes may be as a concept in the study of the historical past, or of contemporary non-Western societies, ... it has become nearly valueless for the interpretation of American society.' As far as he was concerned, the question was 'whether a concept drawn historically from the structure of

Dilemmas and Contradictions in Social Theory

pre-industrial, predemocratic, pre-rationalized society can be of significant help in the clarification (sic) of such a society as ours is today.'[1] More recently, we have other prominent American sociologists attesting vigorously to the 'declining significance of race'; that social **class** has become more important than **race** in determining Black life-chances in America.[2] At one stage in American history class is defunct; at another stage it is race which has declined in significance. Nothing better illustrates the sorry state of sociology; nothing reveals quite as sharply the contradictions and dilemmas in modern social theory. One wonders what next will soon become fashionable.

Wilson's thesis on the declining significance of race is that racism is no longer the factor which excludes Blacks from higher status and higher income positions. The problems of Black life-chances in America, according to Wilson, can all be understood in class terms, not racial terms. This particular thesis does violence both to history and to sociology. For Black people in the New World, and especially in America and Canada, we have to comprehend their historical legal and political status, in addition to their relationship to the means of production, which establishes their **class** position. The former has always been tied to crude ideas about 'race,' so that the important structural issues in American society have to do, as Myrdal[3] and Cox[4] long ago recognized, not simply with **class**. This explains why in the Canadian case, for instance, despite their higher educational and occupational levels as compared to other Canadians, the income levels for Blacks remain low. Many studies repeatedly report discrimination against Blacks in jobs, promotions, housing and social services.[5] As we shall discuss later, this pattern is even more pronounced in the U.S.A.

One of the major reasons why our understanding of Black society is so very limited and sociologically inadequate is that we have not understood certain things about capitalism as a structure of social relations. For example, that capitalism creates two distinct types of division of labor: the one economic; the other social, is not often fully recognized. The social division of labor, such as that which splits the labor market along race-ethnic and gender lines is an issue which sociologists will have to come to grips with, if they are not to create unnecessary blind spots in their analyses. These phenomena are quite different

Understanding of Black Society in North America from class divisions.

The fact that Blacks came to the New World under a special set of circumstances is also not fully recogized or appreciated by sociologists when they discuss the problem of ethnic mobility. Precisely because of these special circumstances, the nature of the disprivilege experienced by Blacks is **unlike** that faced by any other group: 'racial,' linguistic, ethnic or religious. The institutions, culture, and life-styles of Blacks in this hemisphere reflect their peculiar history, a history in which dishonored identities and roles, once imposed upon them, continue to influence their present status and prospects in ways fundamentally different from any other.

Following upon this is a common error of standard sociology: confusing **class disprivilege**, as experienced by many minority groups, with **racial dishonor**, which is the Black experience. Accordingly, it is often assumed that Blacks in the New World face the same set of problems as the Irish, Italians, Poles, Jews, or other European immigrant groups.[6] Such an a-historical, and a-sociological viewpoint says nothing of the racial factor. In fact, it implicitly dismisses that factor, and takes us that much further away from an historically grounded and a sociologically relevant understanding of Blacks in the Americas. It is important to put this in proper historical perspective.

In the U.S.A., **no other group** besides Blacks had Jim Crow laws passed against them, affecting every facet of their lives, and enforced with rigorous brutality. Some sociologists argue, in fact, that in some ways the Jim Crow system was an even more efficient instrument of domination and subordination than slavery had been, and in some ways as difficult to bear psychologically as slavery had been. The reasons are not hard to grasp. **No other group** had to struggle, against unspeakable odds, for basic civil rights which others enjoyed. **No other group** had to live with the reality that the highest Court in the land supported and fully sanctioned a post-slavery servitude by handing down rulings which officially institutionalized and legitimized educational apartheid and racial oppression, essentially establishing the pre-Civil War value of white supremacy and domination. In effect, for Black Americans, a form of mortification analogous to slavery persisted, with official support, for a full hundred years after the Civil War.

Dilemmas and Contradictions in Social Theory

It was only after the Civil Rights protest of the 1960s that Blacks could begin to feel that at last some of their basic rights might be addressed by the rest of the society of which they had been a part.

Consider this, also. Slavery, as a relation of domination in the extreme might have been formally ended in 1865. But between that date and the time the Supreme Court enunciated its doctrine of 'separate but equal' in the 1896 case of **Plessy v. Ferguson,** Black life was only marginally different from what it was in pre-Civil War America. The Black Codes saw to that. Equality for Blacks was still a dream. It took another **two generations** after 1896 for the same level of court to overturn the principle of 'separate but equal.' The 1954 ruling in the case of **Brown v. Board of Education** was supposed to end the dual system of separate but manifestly unequal education, but **defacto** discrimination did not end simply because **dejure** discrimination was overturned. Racism has been for Blacks, as for no other group in the New World, the permanent descant of their lives.

In those critical years between the end of the Civil War in 1865 and the 1954 Supreme Court ruling, the civil rights of Black people in America counted for little. Indeed, historians have argued that public sentiments rather than concern for 'justice' influenced the Court's decision concerning the rights of Blacks and their status in American life. Having lived with the reality of officially sanctioned racism, after 1954 Blacks had to literally devote all of their energies to fighting for basic rights which all other 'immigrant' groups in America had taken for granted.

By the same token, the institution of the sharecropping system in the South after the Civil War **by law** locked the Blacks into a system of **de facto** debt peonage, highly lucrative to the plantation landlords, but utterly demoralizing for the Blacks. Such laws, coupled with the planters' control over state officials, effectively precluded Blacks from independent farming and, in the extreme, prevented them from migrating from the South. This semifeudal social system, it has often been remarked, proved to be even more profitable for the Southern plantocracy than the former slave system. Northern capital, which fully financed this policy, had more than a hint of interest in keeping the Black population in the South in this neo-feudalism.

Understanding of Black Society in North America

Finally, the period between 1900 and 1914 witnessed the most intensive racial hostility against Blacks in all parts of the United States. It was, indeed, a period that crystallized caste relations between Black and White, at the same time as it afforded various privileges such as skilled and better-paying jobs to European immigrant workers. The point is that the disenfranchisement of Blacks, and the entrenchment of their powerlessness, were santioned by law. The coming of the First World War meant simply that Blacks were free to leave the South. In practice, they were free to be exploited in the North as well as in the South.

All told, the last years of the nineteenth century and the early part of the twentieth century up to the First World War, riveted Blacks into a caste status and underclass position, premised on the ideological definition of their Blackness. European immigrants, unencumbered by such structural impediments, sought and gained social, political and economic advancement. How can it be said that Black Americans are just like the immigrant groups? Whatever gains Blacks have made since the Civil War have come slowly, and against structural odds, and much of what is of any substance came only after the 1960s Civil Rights and Black Power protests. And even now in the 1980s, the New Right and the Moral Majority, influential elements in contemporary American politics, are seeking to reverse the progressive social and political initiatives gained by Blacks since 1954. President Reagan's 1983 dismantling of the U.S. Commission on Civil Rights is hardly an action that can bring comfort to those who have been struggling for years for better conditions for Blacks and other minorities. Racism, in short, is endemic in all American institutions, from the Constitution down. What is perhaps more sinister and disturbing about the racism in contemporary politics in the United States is that the New Right has developed forms of ideological discourse that can exploit racist sentiments without giving the appearance of doing so.

II

The foregoing discussion was undertaken in order to underscore the point that only someone who is sociologically blind, or who lacks the slightest shred of historical sensibility could conclude that Black

Dilemmas and Contradictions in Social Theory

Americans are not otherwise different from the various European immigrant groups who have attained social, economic, and political integration in the United States since the turn of the century. Only someone who reads the history of ideas backwards could pretend that the values which underpinned Jim Crowism were not significant for Blacks. Sociologists are fond of reciting in Introductory textbooks that values underpin norms, and that when a norm is applied it is always in order to uphold some value. Laws **are** norms, formal ones. Jim Crow laws were norms, so were the Supreme Court laws. What values do such sociologists suppose these norms sustained? In fact, the Supreme Court already provided the answer to this question in the **Dred Scott** decision of 1857, that critical period prior to the Civil War. The decision, we may know, not only legally opened all American territories to slavery, but it also held that Blacks were inferior to whites and 'could be justly and lawfully be reduced to slavery for his benefit.' Besides, the judges argued then, Blacks had no rights which the white man was bound to respect.

That Blacks in America are in the background, and are relative latecomers in the achievement of basic human and civil rights, has less to do with their class position in American capitalism than with their racial or social position in American society. Similarly, in Canada, the position of Blacks owes more to ideological factors than to economic ones, as the cases of Black domestic workers and the discrimination suffered by Black professionals show.[7]

The concept of race, then, is still central to the structural understanding of the position of Black people, because race has historically been built into the definition of underprivileged situations to which Blacks were thought to naturally belong. Such situations do not depend on the presence of Black people alone; but being Black reinforces disprivilege. It is the existence of the racial factor which explains why, in the United States, there was no equivalent in **class** stratification to the racial codes and Jim Crow laws which characterized the post-Bellum South. More than the residues of such a caste structure persist to this day.

Racial ideology is quintessentially cultural, learned in society as a part of ideational culture. It is one of the key lessons from the sociology of knowledge that ideas, once expressed, become public

174

Understanding of Black Society in North America

property and form the basis for stable social relationships, whatever the nature of those relationships, whatever the nature of those ideas. Ideas also have a way of persisting long after the conditions that gave birth to them have disappeared. Those of us interested in understanding the structure of social relations which decisively affect Black life in the western hemisphere will do well to take some insights from the sociology of knowledge. As that area of study which raises questions about the nature of knowledge as a social product (that is, its social determinants) and about the consequences of such knowledge or idea-system, it constitutes an integral component of any worthwhile sociology, including in this case, the sociology of Black society in the New World.

For Blacks, the one idea-system which has been the keystone of their lives, the central ideology on which all else depends, is white racism. Such racism is more than attitude; it is to be conceptualized as a **relationship**. Given the fact that it is the permanent undercurrent in every institution in the United States, its practice, above all else, has provided the basis for the centuries-long tradition of struggle among Black people. The legal and then customary barrier drawn between Black and White in the United States continues to have structural importance in the society. The situation in Canada closely parallels this.

In fact, the concept of **racial oppression** has recently been suggested as being not an inappropriate one for analyzing the position of Blacks in North American society as a whole. As Bolaria and Li put it in their recent important book, in its extreme form, racial oppression is not only a fact of life, but also a part of the **statutory system** which helps to legalize and thereby perpetuate it. Ideological control is at the core of racial oppression. It is a means to indoctrinate the defined subordinate group to be servile.[8] These authors cite the case of Black domestic workers in Canada whose tenuous **legal** status in this country[9] leaves them extremely vulnerable to exploitation, and in effect reinforces the ideological image of the Black Sambo - docile, compliant and obedient. We must insist that Blacks have (and always have had in the North American diaspora) a specific **ideological**, as well as **economic**, existence. Racial stratification is a structural overlay on class stratification.

175

Dilemmas and Contradictions in Social Theory

Black Society, as we know it today in North America, is a **product** of some very brutal social relations of the kind no other group in this hemisphere has encountered to the same degree, and for the same length of time. The circumstances of forced migration from Africa to the New World, slavery and servitude in the plantation economies of the hemisphere, and the subsequent structural ramifications of caste stratification and class disprivilege in the national societies in which Blacks currently live, are the stuff of a sociology of Black society. The combination of all these experiences **in one group**, is unique to Blacks.

III

This chapter concludes with a brief discussion of the second problem identified previously - the narrowing of the gap between Blacks and Whites. Again, we face contradictions that clearly reflect a failure of sociologists to understand the historical significance of the social relations revolving around the large-scale exploitation of unfree labor for profit maximization.

The formal ending of slavery in the United States after the Civil War, and the different Supreme Court rulings ordering desegregation of public facilities, appeared on the surface to have been the signal that Blacks in the U.S. had at last been allowed equal opportunities to compete for the rewards of society. But this was nothing more than a grand illusion. The fact is that in the United States, as elsewhere in the Americas, institutional racism and structural discrimination against Blacks have provided formidable obstacles to equality. As one of Wilson's critics has noted, in all major respects: from housing to school defacto segregation, and income levels, most Blacks are in a severely disadvantaged position when compared to Whites.[10] And they are in that position because of the persistence of large-scale **racial** inequality in the different spheres of Black life in America. In present discriminatory practices involving the recruitment practices of employers, promotion practices, lay-off and seniority practices, and housing discrimination practices, can be found the manifestation of racial ideology, **not class disprivilege**. Ironically, Wilson himself also says that 'one of the legacies of the

Understanding of Black Society in North America

racial oppression in previous years is the continued disproportionate Black representation in the underclass.'[11]

The hard fact, then, is that the historical circumstances of Black servitude in America, and its structural consequences are felt by Black Americans in the 1980s. Almost any source which one consults, reveals the same picture. In American society, much inequality and discrimination against Blacks remains, whether one uses such measures as unemployment rates, income levels, or education. As indicated in the table below, one economist has calculated that in certain key measures of well-being, Blacks in American society lag far behind whites.[12]

Years Blacks are Behind Whites

Indicator of Well-Being	Approximate Number of Years that Blacks Are behind Whites
Income	30
Employment	50 or more
Education	over 20
Housing	20 to 30
Health	from 20 to 30
Wealth	over 100

Source: Jhabzala, 1977, p. 159.

Recent official U.S. Federal statistics amply confirm this picture as well. As of 1980, Black families earned 59 per cent of white income, or fifty-nine dollars for every hundred dollars earned by white families.[13] Not all of this disparity is due to differences in education, or work experience. Farley reports from his calculations, that even if all Black male workers had the same characteristics as white male workers in 1974, the Black workers still would have earned an average of $2,271 less per year.[14]

The simple truth of American society is that, in absolute terms, Blacks have gained. But **in relative terms,** (which is where it really matters) Blacks remain far behind whites in the crucial areas of higher education, income, political office holding and upper-level occupations. In relative terms, there has

177

Dilemmas and Contradictions in Social Theory

been practically no change in the position of Blacks and whites since the Second World War, and the gains, where they can be detected over the past several decades, can best be described as modest. The gap is still very large, when we look at virtually any indicator of general welfare, and discrimination still accounts for much of the difference.

In the U.S., where approximately 12 percent (or 26 million) of the population are Black Americans, their life-chances still lag far behind whites, especially in the economic sector, and Blacks remain among the most disadvantaged group in American society. According to a U.S. News and World Report of August 1981, Blacks' income in that year was 56.2% of whites, down from 60.3% ten years earlier.

Even more recent, extensive studies utilizing techniques of demographic measurement to analyze Census Bureau data, deliver mixed conclusions. The conclusions are inevitably mixed because the 'progress' which Blacks have made is not the across-the-board type. Furthermore, the opinions on the subject divide easily into three: the optimists who believe that skin color now has little to do with opportunity chances in America; the pessimists, who see more of the superficiality and pseudo nature of what passes for progress; and a third view which sees Blacks as increasingly polarized into a successful elite group, and a downtrodden underclass.[15]

The most general conclusion drawn from current sociological research is that although Blacks have made some gains economically, politically and in educational achievements, there are still many barriers to social equality, and such barriers are rooted in patterns and practices of racial discrimination that are deeply entrenched and well-institutionalized in the very structure of American society, at the highest levels. In establishing a 'scoreboard on Black progress,' Farley reminds us that 'throughout the nation's history there has been a tendency to underestimate the magnitude of racial differences, to overestimate the progress that has been made, and to oversimplify the solutions to the remaining racial problems.' He therefore warns against focusing upon the gains and subscribing to the assumption that the time has come for a strategy of benign neglect.

What the evidence has quite clearly shown is that,

Understanding of Black Society in North America

inspite of a movement toward racial equality, there is still a long distance to go. 'Black men are still twice as likely as white men to be out of work... a high and growing proportion of Black families have incomes below the poverty line' (24% higher than for whites). Farley concludes '... the public schools in New York, Chicago, Los Angeles, Philadelphia, and Washington were as **racially** segregated in 1980 as two decades earlier. Much remains to be done before we will be able to say unequivocally that the economic and social gap between the races has been closed.'[16]

In Canada, much if not all, of the inequality between Blacks and Whites can be attrituted to the racial factor, and such inequality cannot be explained by denying the racial factor. Blacks have been in Canada since the early seventeenth Century. Their long presence in Canada notwithstanding, the discrimination which they face, based on 'race,' relegates them to conditions of marginality, as in Nova Scotia, or to the status of undesirables, as in the case of Black taxi drivers in Montreal. Their marginal situation and their defined undesirable status, are premised on structural variables rooted in a society with a covert, but unmistakable racism. As sociologists Clairmont and Magill explain, it is impossible to understand either the contemporary socio-economic condition of Black Nova Scotians without recognizing that Nova Scotia was at one time a 'slave society,' and without appreciating the conditions of immigration and settlement of free Blacks in that province.[17]

The groundwork for the subordination of the Blacks as a people in Nova Scotia was laid by the early existence of a slave society, which in time institutionalized the oppression of Blacks, and fostered attitudes of White superiority. The historical legacy of such oppression and attitudes are no longer confined to Nova Scotia, and Blacks in all the metropolitan centres in Canada continue to experience racial intolerance and blatant discrimination derived from long-standing negative attitudes toward them as a group.[18]

In Canada, the ideology of racism has served as a structural barrier to the employment of Blacks, including professional Blacks. Recent findings suggest that because of racism, in the Canadian job market whites have three job prospects to every one for Blacks. As Frances Henry found in her study of

Dilemmas and Contradictions in Social Theory

metropolitan Toronto, the area in Canada with the largest concentration of non-whites, there is deep-seated and widespread racism, cutting across religion, age, and social status of the white population.[19] The racism in Canada may be 'polite' racism, as Hughes and Kallen put it,[20] but it is still racism, and for those who are the ultimate victims of this ideology and practice, it is no less devastating and demoralizing than the overt expressions of racism found elsewhere.

IV

The problem with racial injustice in North America is that the level of racial ideology is so deep that its gravity is not fully recognized. To the dominant group, discrimination based on racial criteria must be like breathing-in and breathing-out: 'second nature.' The ideology permeates such potentially progressive and liberal elements of the society as the labor, socialist and women's movements.[21]

Understanding Black society demands that one grasps how and why particular perceptions of, and beliefs about, racial differences came to be institutionalized in every corner of the Black Diaspora. The widespread and intransigent racial dogma which has shaped the quality of Black people's lives in this hemisphere is best approached in a comparative frame of reference. The effort of the sociological imagination involves the employment of a historical sensibility, and a realization that many of the problems that currently plague the Black community in the New World can be traced to the effects of the plantation/colonial experience which lasted for two and a half centuries in the New World. Proper historical reckoning is indispensable in social study, and it immeasurably enhances both interpretive and comparative understanding.

It takes a critical mind to note the key theoretical point that racism in North America has not diminished; it has simply been camouflaged by the rhetoric of liberal ideology. More to the point, racism has been joined by other ideologies of the Right such as patriarchy, and the anti-ERA and anti-busing campaigns of recent years. The lawsuits challenging Affirmative Action (Bakke, Weber) attest to the

Understanding of Black Society in North America

continuing significance of race as a political force in American society and other parts of the New World.

Much of the standard literature on Black Society is unsatisfactory from a theoretical point of view because it ignores the ideological and macro variables such as racism, and focuses on individualistic 'problems' which do not, in themselves, necessarily shed light on the larger historical realities that decisively define what happens at the level of biography. As C. Wright Mills long ago reminded us, neither the life of the individual nor the history of a society can be understood without understanding both. The special ability advocated by Mills - the **sociological imagination** - enables us to grasp history and biography and the relations between the two within society. And no social study that does not come back to the problems of biography, of history and of their intersections within society has completed its intellectual journey.[22]

Racism, sexism, class oppression/deception, the pillage of the Third World and ideological faith-healing are all major societal problems in modern society. To the degree that these problems have been given distinctly theoretical analyses, such analyses have often overlooked the theoretical significance of providing an interpretation which links these problems to larger historical nets of social arrangements. These problems are not individual problems. They incubate in social structure; more precisely in capitalism as a structure of social relations.

If we are to continue to call ourselves sociologists, or social scientists, or students of society, we must get beyond the common superficial accounts of these human experiences. The essays in this book have provided the structural understanding of societal processes, and have demonstrated, with ample illustrations, how ordinary citizens are caught up in the abstract, and seemingly natural and inevitable nets of social arrangements. Critical social theory understands that no social arrangement is inevitable. This is perhaps one of the most important insights into society which social theory can offer. When that is grasped, it will be seen more clearly that men and women do make history (some men and women more than others). But this history, nevertheless, becomes oppressive, not in an anthropomorphic sense, but because human beings make it so. If we fail to

181

Dilemmas and Contradictions in Social Theory

understand that the social and cultural world is the world we have made, we have no basis for wanting to change it. It would, indeed, be an unnecessary tragedy if we cannot change what we have made.

Understanding of Black Society in North America

NOTES

1. Robert Nisbet, **Tradition and Revolt**, New York: 1968; and **idem.**, "The decline and fall of social classes," **Pacific Sociological Review**, vol. II, 1959, pp. 11-17. See, also, Arnold Rose, "The concept of class and American sociology," **Social Research**, vol. 15, 1958, pp. 53-59 and Wilbert E. Moore, "But some are more equal than others," **American Sociological Review**, vol. 28, 1963, pp. 14-15.

2. William J. Wilson, **The Declining Significance of Race**, Chicago: University of Chicago Press, 1978.

3. Gunnar Myrdal, **An American Dilemma: The Negro Problem and Modern Democracy**, New York: Harper and Row Publishers, 1944.

4. Oliver Cromwell Cox, **Caste, Class and Race: A Study in Social Dynamics**, New York: Monthly Review Press, 1948.

5. See, for example, B. Singh Bolaria and Peter S. Li, **Racial Oppression in Canada**, Toronto: Garamond Press, 1985, p. 181; and Frances Henry, "The demographic correlates of racism in Toronto," in **Black Presence in Multi-Ethnic Canada**, ed. V. Doyley, Vancouver, B.C.: U.B.C. Faculty of Education, 1978.

6. See, for instance, Irving Kristol, "The Negro today is like the immigrant of yesterday," in **Nation of Nations: The Ethnic Experience and the Racial Crises**, ed. Peter I. Rose, New York: Random House, 1972; and Nathan Glazer, "Black and ethnic groups: the difference and the political difference it makes," **Social Problems**, 18 (Spring) 1971, pp. 444-61.

7. Bolaria and Li, **op.cit.**; and Henry, **op.cit.** See, also, Rachel Epstein, "Domestic workers: the experience in B.C.," in Linda Brishin and Linda Yanz (eds.), **Union Sisters: Women in the Labor Movement**, Toronto: The Women's Press, 1983, pp. 222-237; and Makeda Silvera, **Silenced** (Talks with Working Class West Indian Women about their Lives and Struggles as Domestic Workers in Canada). Toronto: Williams-Wallace Pub. Inc., 1983.

Dilemmas and Contradictions in Social Theory

8. Bolaria and Li, **op.cit.**, pp. 17, 179 (emphasis added).

9. **Ibid.**

10. Charles Willie, "The inclining significance of race," **Society**, (July-August) 1978, pp. 10-15. Also, see Willie (ed.), **The Caste and Class Controversy**, Bayside: General Hall, 1979; cf. David Edgar, "Reagan's hidden agenda: racism and the American right," **Race and Class**, vol. 22, #3, 1981, pp. 221-38.

11. Wilson, **op.cit.**, p. 19.

12. Firdous Jhabzala, "The economic situation of Black people," in **Problems in Political Economy: An Urban Perspective**, 2nd ed., Lexington, Mass.: David Gorden, 1977, pp. 153-160.

13. See, for example, U.S. Bureau of the Census, **Statistical Abstracts of the U.S., 1982-1983**, Washington, D.C., p. 404; U.S. Bureau of the Census, **The Social and Economic Status of the Black Population in the U.S.: An Historical View, 1790-1978**, Washington, D.C.: Government Printing Office, 1979, p. 69; and **idem.**, 1981.

14. Reynolds Farley, "Trends in racial inequalities: have the signs of the 1960s disappeared in the 1970s?" **American Sociological Review**, 42 (April), 1977, pp. 189-208. In a more dramatic fashion, it has been suggested that Blacks do not even get a fair share of life itself, since their average life span is seven years less than that of whites. The Black man lives about 15 years less on average than white females; Black babies are less likely than white babies to survive their first year. More Black women die during pregnancy and childbirth than their white cohorts. When convicted of similar crimes, Blacks get longer prison sentences than those given to whites. Charles Anderson and Jeffry Gibson, **Toward a New Sociology** (Third Edition), Homewood, Ill.: Dorsey Press, 1978, p. 279.

15. Reynolds Farley, **Blacks and Whites: Narrowing the Gap?**, Cambridge, Mass.: Harvard University Press, 1984.

Understanding of Black Society in North America

16. **Ibid.**, p. 206 (emphasis added).

17. Don Clairmont and Dennis Magill, **Africville: The Life and Death of a Canadian Black Community,** Toronto: McLelland and Stewart, 1974.

18. See the survey undertaken by the **Montreal Gazette,** April 10, 12, 13, 14, 15, 16, 1982, published in G. Llewellyn Watson (ed.), **Black Society in the Americas: Essays in Comparative Sociology,** Lexington, Mass.: Ginn Press, 1986.

19. Henry, **op.cit.**

20. See David Hughes and Evelyn Kallen, **The Anatomy of Racism: Canadian Dimensions,** Montreal: Harvester House, 1974, p. 214.

21. Robert Allen, **Reluctant Reformers,** Washington, D.C.: Howard University Press, 1974, pp. 224-247.

22. C. Wright Mills, **The Sociological Imagination,** New York: Oxford University Press, 1959, pp. 3, 6.

INDEX

Adorno, Theodor, 54, 88, 109
Advertising, as culture industry, 88-90
Agribusinesses, multinational, 133
Althusser, Louis, 11, 109, 120, 121
Assumptions, Marxian, on patriarchy, 19
Austin, J.L., 58

Beechey, Veronica, 24
Bell, Daniel, 102
Benjamin, Walter, 54

Capitalism, world, 131-148; and inequality, 144; and the split labor market, 170
Commodities, fetishism of, 90-92
Competence, communicative (Habermas), 58
Comte, A., 1
Consciousness, reified, 7
Consumerism, terror of, 89-92
Consensus, orthodox, ix, 51-52, 160
Consumption, mindless, 91-92
Contradictions, in capitalist relations, 79-88; in global political economy, 141; in social theory, 149-150, 156-161, 176
Coser, Lewis, 150
Cox, Oliver C., 157
Craib, Ian, xii, xiii
Crisis, in understanding, 3, 13; in liberalism, 4; in Marxism, 7-11; rationality/economic, 82; legitimation, 82-83; motivation, 83
Conflicts and protest, in the sixties, 50, 172

Critical theory: (see also Frankfurt School), 53-61, 134, 141, 143, 156-158, 162-163, 181; theoretical sources of, 55-59; program of, 67-103; and critique of positivism, 68-71; and disbelief in proletarian revolution, 72; and critique of Marxism, 71-77; and critique of modern capitalist society, 77-103; and critique of culture industry, 88-90; and critique of ideology, 92-95; and critique of science and technology, 95-103; neglect of, in North America, 156-158; Summary chart of, 62
Critique, theoretical, of capitalist society, xiv
Culture, of critical discourse, (Gouldner), 76-77, 159, 160

Davis, Arthur K., 13-14
Debt peonage, de facto, 172
Dialectics, Marxian, 55
Discrimination, racial, 178
Dishonor, racial, and the Black experience, 171
Disprivilege, class, and the Black experience, 171
Domestics, Black, in Canada 18n, 174, 175
Dominant ideology, of Canada, Liberalism, 118
Domination, critique of, 54-58; male, and patriarchal

values, 25, 26;
of women, 10

Economics, bourgeois, 15;
ideology of, 98
Economic theory, liberal,
102-103
Eisenstein, Zillah, 24, 26
Ellul, Jacques, 97
Engels, F., 9, 26, 71
Epistemology, and sociology,
153
Ethnomethodology, 149, 151,
153, 155;
critics' reaction to, 150,
155;
requirements of, 153;
as anti-positivist, 53

Farley, Reynolds, 178-179
Feminism, power of, 30;
and F. Engels, 19, 39n;
Feminist, fallacy, 26;
critique of patriarchy,
29, 31, 33
Firestone, Shulsmith, 21
Frankfurt School: (see also
critical theory), 8, 10,
30, 32, 67ff, 74, 99, 119;
and critique of
positivism, 68-71;
and critique of Marxism,
71-77;
on ideology, 118
French, M., 137
Freudian psycho-analysis, as
related to critical
theory, 56, 95
Fromm, Erich, 54
Functionalism, 50, 51
Functionalist sociologists,
49, 50

Garfinkel, Harold, 149-150,
155
Giddens, Anthony, 121
Gouldner, Alvin, xvi, 70,
76-77, 100, 159-160
Gramsci, Antonio, 74, 109;
on dominant (hegemonic)
ideology, 117
Grove, Walter, 152
Grunberg, Carl, 54

Habermas, Jurgen: (see also
Frankfurt School), 30, 54,
56;
on linguistic philosophy,
58;
on critical theory, 59;
on communications and
distortions, 60, 100;
and critique of
positivism, 68;
on the proletariat, 72;
on critique of ideology,
95;
meta-theoretical scheme
of, 99;
on ideology, 121
Harassment, sexual, and
patriarchy, 28;
of working women, 26
Harrison, Paul, 123
Hartmann, Heidi, 20
Henry, Frances, 179
Hermeneutics, 55, 56;
double, 154
Home-sewing, in Canada, 17n
Horkheimer, Max, 30, 54, 68,
88

Ideology, as social
discourse, 109-130;
in patriarchy, 21, 22, 23,
31;
capitalist, 31, 39n, 98,
126, 131;
'end of ideology thesis',
49, 52;
in sociology, xvi;
critique of, 92-95;
at the formal level of
schooling, 38n;
liberal, 12, 118, 119;
of multinational
corporations, 15;
racist, 169;
dominant, 22, 93, 112,
114, 118, 125;

differing conceptions of, 109-110;
definition of, 110;
as integrated belief system, 110;
as psychological distortion, 110;
Karl Marx's conception of, 111-116;
bourgeois, 111;
ruling class, 113-114;
and science, 114, 120-121, 165n;
Karl Mannheim's conception of, 116-117;
Antonio Gramsci's conception of, 117-120;
hegemonic, 117-118, 124, 125;
counter, 119, 120;
as distorted communications, 119;
Louis Althusser's theory of, 120-123;
as culture, 124-125;
racial, 174, 175, 180;
racial, and inequality, 176, 177

Janeway, Elizabeth, 25
Jim Crow laws, as instruments of domination, 171; as formal norms, 174

Kant, I., 5
Kellner, D., 124, 125
Knowledge, types of, and interests (Habermas), 100-101, 153;
as a commodity, 58;
Summary chart of, 101
Korsch, Karl, 74
Kuhn, Thomas, 152

Labor, ontology of (Marxian) 57, 134, 143;
of Third World people, 132;
price of, 134
Language, ordinary

(Habermas), 58
Leiss, William, 97
Liberal theory, 5, 10-12;
critique of, 15;
on economics, 102
Lipset, Seymour, 49
Lukacs, Georg, 30, 74

Mannheim, Karl, 22, 109, 116-117
Marchak, Pat, 116, 118, 119
Marcuse, Herbert, 30, 54, 68;
on commodity fetishism, 91;
on ideology, 96
Marx, Karl, 6, 7, 9, 10, 14, 24, 60, 149;
assumptions of, 19;
against Feuerbach, 25;
dialectical analysis of, 67;
analysis of the capitalist state, 85;
on ideology, 22, 23, 93, 109-121;
on social change, 136
Marxian, concepts, 3;
theory, 3, 7, 10, 12, 28, 32;
insights, 32-34;
theory of ideology, 111;
theory of capitalism, 134, 142
Marxist, scholarship, 3;
sociology, 8-9
Marxism, 6-7, 20, 28, 71-77;
as social theory, 36, 73;
and self-evaluation, 74
Media, and consumption imagery, 93
Merton, R., 46
Meta-sociology, aspects of, 61
Meta-theory, as anti-positivist, 155, 161, 45ff, 53
Miliband, Ralph, 11
Mills, C. Wright, 50, 181
Multinational corporations, and Third World countries,

2, 123, 137;
in Brazil, 135, 142;
and wage labor, 138-139, 142;
and unemployment, 134, 137, 140, 141

Neumann, Franz, 54
New class, Gouldner's, 76-77
Nisbet, Robert, 169

O'Connor, James, 11, 86
Oppression, racial, and the analysis of Blacks in North America, 175
Ortner, Sherri, 25
Osler, Margaret, 122

Paradigms, in sociology, 46
Parsons, Talcott, 48, 49, 52;
and functionalism, 50, 51, 53;
neglect of critical theory, 156
Patriarchy, 19ff, 35n;
and Marxian theory, 19, 20, 24, 28, 29, 32, 33;
and feminist theory, 31;
as domination, 20, 21, 24, 27, 28, 32;
as sexual exploitation, 20;
and biology thesis, 24-26;
and domestic work, 21;
and the double-day, 26, 27;
and capitalism, 20, 24, 27, 29, 41ff, 42n;
as a system of power, 20, 34, 41n;
origins of, 26-27
Pharmaceutical companies, multinational, 123, 140
Phenomenology, 53, 57, 154
Philosophy, linguistic, 57-58
Politics, the mystification of, 58, 59
Pollock, Friedrich, 54
Popper, Karl, 69, 150, 151
Positivism, and critical theory, 45ff, 59;
assumptions of, 45-48, 70-71;
definition of, 46;
and reification, 70
Positivists, modern day, 1, 48
Poulantzas, Nicos, 11
Proletariat, in modern capitalism, 72;
as (failed) agents of social transformation, 8

Race, as a central concept in the sociology of Black people, 174
Race, declining significance of (according to William Wilson), 170
Racial ideology, 174, 175, 179, 180
Racism, in contemporary America, 173, 181;
as the central ideology in Black/White relationship, 175;
in Canada, 179-180
Rationality, capitalist, 5, 132-133
Reification, 7, 15, 112
Rich, Adrienne, 21

Sarte, J.P., 5
Sayers, Janet, 20, 21, 25
Science, method of, 122;
content of, 122;
in sociology, 150;
social features of, 151-153
Science and technology, critique of, 95-103
Secombe, Wally, 21
Sewart, John, 76
Shor, Ira, 160
Slavery, as a relation of domination, 172
Social class, irrelevance of (according to Robert Nisbet), 169-170
Social events, difference

from natural phenomena, 154
Social issues, and sociology, ix
Social question, and sociology, 1-2
Social theory, as medium of enlightenment, ix, xv-xvi;
  its failure to reveal, xii;
  as creating mystique, xii;
  as being in a paradoxical situation, xiii
Social theory, essential task of, 23;
  as an interpretive or hermeneutic process, 56;
  as reflection upon society, 161;
  its importance, xiv;
  its goal, xiv;
  and its two dialectics, xv;
  historical nature of, 162
Sociologists, humanist, 155
Sociology of knowledge, 111
Sociology, 'conflict', 51;
  lifelessness of, x;
  as positivist science, 1;
  as critical discourse on politics and society, 1;
  liberal, 2;
  mainstream, in North America, 48;
  critical, 52;
  radical, 53;
  fragmentation of, 149;
  positivist, 52-53;
  in Canada, 52;
  findings of, 153;
  and values, 153-154;
  as a critique of society, 159
Statism, 11, 78-88;
  state intervention, 12, 71;
  Capitalist, and contradictions, 78ff;
  and the dominant class, 84-88;
  fiscal crisis of, 85;
  Canadian, 85, 86
Sumner, Colin, 115
Synthesis, theoretical, in sociology, 60;
  dialectical (Habermas), 100
Szymanski, Al, 27

Theory, liberal economic, 6;
  liberal, 5, 10, 13, 15
Theoretical system, Marxian, 6, 7
Third World, and multinational corporations, 96, 132-144, 145n
Toffler, Alvin, 5
Turner, Jonathan, 157

Veblen, Thorstein, 159

Walton, John, 140, 141
Weber, Max, 5, 149;
  on liberalism, 5;
  on hermeneutics, 55;
  on verstehen, 56
Wilson, William, 170, 176
Winch, Peter, 58
Wittgenstein, Ludwig, 58

ABOUT THE AUTHOR

G. Llewellyn Watson is Associate Professor of Sociology in the University of Prince Edward Island, Canada. Educated at the University of York in England, (B.A., D.Phil.) and the University of Guelph, (M.A.), Dr. Watson is the author of the highly acclaimed **Social Theory and Critical Understanding**, (1982). He edited **Black Society in the New World: Essays in Comparative Sociology**, 1986, and is co-editing with Aubrey W. Bonnett (Hunter College, CUNY) **Essays on the Black Diaspora: New World Perspectives.** Dr. Watson's many essays have been published in major social science journals in North America and England, and he has just completed two major works: (1) 'Jamaican Sayings: A Study in Folklore, Aesthetics and Social Control'; and (2) a Bibliographic study on 'Feminism and Women's Issues.' His current research interest is in Tourism.